Heaven's Homecoming

FATHER DOUGLAS McKAY

This book is dedicated to my Mother and Father
Agnes Mary and Harry Joseph McKay
who first instilled the Catholic faith into my heart
and in loving memory
of the Holy Family Home residents,
who lived and died under my priestly watch.

Author's Note:

Heaven's Homecoming is a sacred book based on
the community of Holy Family Home about the
Indwelling Presence of God and His transforming
love for us; it is in the spirit of Saint Jeanne Jugan
and her Little Sisters of the Poor; and it is
recommended that only a chapter a day be read
before prayer time to drink in and savor the wisdom
of the aged, our beloved little elders. The names are
fictitious, but the stories are truthful.

HOLY FAMILY HOME, PHILADELPHIA, PENNSYLVANIA

ISBN 978-1-4675-342-6

Design: Carol McLaughlin, Saint Joseph's University Creative Services

TABLE OF CONTENTS

FORWARD

A priest is ordained to accompany the Pilgrim People of God in their journey through life. He shares in the hope of Baptisms, the love of weddings, and the faith that sees us through this life into the life to come. It is the joy and the burden of priestly service.

In *Heaven's Homecoming*, Father McKay shares with us some of those moments from his 18 years experience with the Little Sisters of the Poor in Philadelphia. Despite his personal apprehensions—which we all have—as he approaches those who approach eternity, he shares with us the discovery of God's goodness. Through the personalities of those he serves, we find hope when so often there appears to be none. These vignettes are a testament of mercy especially in a world where older people are so easily disregarded and discarded. These are stories of confidence even when fear seems overwhelming.

And as we continue to discover more deeply the mystery of the Communion of Saints, we are also able to see how we discover the great hope to which we are all called. It is in giving of ourselves to those who seem to have so little to give themselves that we find the great treasure of our vocation to holiness.

Heaven's Homecoming celebrates the profound silence of indescribable joy in the presence of our God who calls us home to Himself. Since this is our goal, "let's go on for God...."

+ Timothy M. Dolan
Archbishop of New York

ACKNOWLEDGMENTS

In appreciation for all my helpers who have edited, inspired, and encouraged me in the writing of this sacred book: An Anonymous Backer, Catherine Blithe, Liz Burns, Paul Buzas, Sr. Frances Catherine, lsp, Dr. Raymond Coughlin, Mary Ellen Fattori, Sr. Ann Marie Harrison, IHM, Patricia Lo, Thomas Mahon, Sr. Kateri Nealon, lsp, Paula Paul, Sr. Margaret Regina, lsp, Sr. Elizabeth Teresa, lsp, Mary Walter, the theology class, the residents, the extended community at Holy Family Home, the Little Sisters of the Poor, and, especially, the Holy Spirit.

PROLOGUE

On the first day of summer, June 21st, I began my new assignment as chaplain of Holy Family Home in Southwest Philadelphia. Fourteen Little Sisters of the Poor in white habits surrounded me in the Blue Room of their home where they greeted their guests. There I sat, wearing my Roman collar and priestly suit. Rocking nervously, I blurted out, "I feel like Father O'Malley in *The Bells of Saint Mary's!*" Joyous laughter erupted, and I felt at home.

At the end of our get-acquainted meeting, Sister Amez, the assistant superior, escorted me on the grand tour of the facility. Under blue skies and white clouds, we walked around the garden grounds that were enclosed by a large stone wall. An aging couple strolled, arm-in-arm, gently holding one another up. A distinguished gray-haired man sat on a bench whistling at the bobbing robins in the green grass. Scampering squirrels played tag around the towering trees. Monarch butterflies fluttered above the overflowing triple-tier fountain. Fragrant flowers made me sneeze. And a gentle breeze, like the breath of God, made my spirit soar.

"It's a little paradise," I said to Sister Amez. "Is this heaven?"

"Not quite, Father Christopher, but close to it."

"Please, call me Father Chris; I like it better."

After admiring the garden statues of Saint Joseph, the Sacred Heart of Jesus, the grotto of Lourdes, and the gigantic stone images of Calvary, I humored my religious guide by petting an imaginary dog. In the midst of the colorful flowers, I spun around my unseen pet, remarking, "Toto, I have a feeling we're not in Philadelphia anymore." Sister laughed, as I added, "We must be somewhere over the rainbow."

Just then, the chapel bells rang out. Amusing me, Sister raised her hands in worship, her eyes matching the blue sky and her habit the white clouds. Accompanying the melody of the chimes, she sang out:

> *Then sings my soul,*
> *My Savior God to Thee;*
> *How great Thou art,*
> *How great Thou art!*

Shortly thereafter, we entered the yellowish-brick building. Sister Amez then showed me the library, the TV lounges, the patio, the social hall, the tea room, the dining rooms, and the candy store. Inside the store my cup of joy sweetly overflowed as I spoke to my first resident at Holy Family Home. Anticipating the Fourth of July, she sat in her red, white, and blue decorated clothes. Saluting her, I remarked, "You don't look old enough to live here."

Smiling at me while licking a taffy, she responded, "I'll 'ave ya know, Father, I'm 95."

"Really? What's your secret?" I asked.

"The fountain of youth," she answered, lifting an invisible shot glass between her thumb and index finger. Downing the make-believe whiskey, she smacked her lips with more delight proclaiming, "The fountain of youth, Father, and the Little Sisters of the Poor!"

Saving the best for last, Sister Amez finally ushered me into the chapel. There she left me in the company of our Eucharistic Lord. The sacred candle, consuming itself in the sanctuary, attested to holy ground. The Burning Bush blazed in my mind; I wanted to remove my shoes. Instead, I knelt before the glittering tabernacle and adored the Real Presence of God, praying:

"May the Heart of Jesus, in the Most Blessed Sacrament, be praised, adored, and loved with grateful affection, at every moment, in all the tabernacles of the world, even to the end of time. Amen."

After a few moments, as I stood and turned around to leave, I noticed a Bible in the first pew. Imprinted on its cover appeared the image of the ascended Lord, wearing an alb and a red sash around his waist, standing on rose-tinted clouds amidst angelic trumpeters. Attracted by this inviting scene, I embraced the holy book and sat down. Curiously, I opened it to its marker and read the following highlighted words from John 14:3:

I am indeed going to prepare a place for you,
and then I shall come back to take you with me,
that where I am you also may be.

Eighteen years later, I would see that same attractive Bible again, opened to that very same page. Only this time, it would be on the pall, draped over someone's casket. Little did I know how that highlighted passage would be set like a diploma's seal—not on parchment, though, but rather, on my heart, my priestly heart.

Come now—you are cordially invited—to meet and learn from these spiritual professors of the faith, "the A-B-C Graduates" of Holy Family Home, our guides to *Heaven's Homecoming.*

In the beginning ...

—Genesis 1:1

NGIE
Queen Bride

Just starting my first day at Holy Family Home, I checked my mailbox and found the following note:

> *Dear Pastor Christopher,*
> *Please come and see me. I need you now.*
> *I'm in room 6, Floor 3. Take your time.*
> —*Angie*
>
> *P.S. But hurry up!*

In the hallway, Sister Amez stopped me, saying, "Angie wants to see you."

"I know," I said, biting an apple. "I'll see her after lunch and—" My beeper suddenly blasted! Again—to see Angie. "This poor woman must think she's dying."

"Father, you never know," Sister said. "He may come like a 'thief in the night'. Last year, I remember feeding Peggy, one of our younger residents. She was alert and talkative. After swallowing some of her food, she looked up, pointed down the hallway, radiated a smile, and said, 'Here He comes!' As I held her feeding spoon close to her mouth, she bowed her head and died—

right in front of me—before finishing her meal."

"Sister, that story just gave me goose bumps."

"In here, we call them, 'God Bumps'".

Finishing my apple, I rushed to see Angie. In her room, she sat on her rocking chair, eating cookies, and watching TV. Above her bed, I saw a crucifix. On a small table next to her were cookies, a little plastic angel—with its wings folded down—and a small plaque of Blessed Jeanne Jugan, the foundress of the Little Sisters of the Poor. Greeting her, I said, "Good morning, Angie."

"O, ya must be the new pastor," she said, springing off her rocker.

"Not the pastor, the new chaplain."

"Ya'll do, Father Christopher."

"Please, call me Father Chris; I like it better."

"Whatever."

"Are you sick?" I asked.

"Yeah, I got a headache, but I thank God I got a head."

"That's good," I said. "How about my blessing?"

"Yeah, that's why I called ya—to bless my new Jeanne Jugan," she said, pointing at the image of the canonized saint soon-to-be."

"That's all?" I asked. "I thought you were dying?"

"I am—I'm on my way ta heaven."

After blessing her and the little plaque, I asked, "Angie, what do you know about Jeanne Jugan?"

"I know I wouldn't have my bed without her." She sat down on her mattress. "I like it; it's comfortable."

"What do you mean?" I asked.

"I mean, Jeanne Jugan let a blind lady sleep in her bed while she slept on the floor."

"But what's that got to do with your bed?"

"Well, when she gave up her bed, God was so pleased that He

multiplied her bed 70 times, 70 times, including mine and yours. That's how we got the Little Sisters, ya know. Got it now?"

"I'm not sure," I said.

"Ya better talk to the Sisters, Father; they know the whole story."

"I will."

The next day, as I walked off the elevator, I saw roly-poly Angie sitting on the bench, next to the chapel.

"Are ya waiting for the bus?" I asked.

"Yeah, ya mean the one for heaven, right?"

"Yeah, that's the one."

"It's coming, Father. Do ya wanna git aboard wit me?"

"No, I'm not ready. But you are."

"Not today. I gotta git all dressed up first," she said, smiling.

"Why are you always smiling, Angie?" I ask. "Tell me your secret."

"Cus, I'm on my way ta heaven and that makes me happy."

"But aren't you afraid to die?"

"No, I'm afraid I won't die soon enough."

Another time when she sat on her favorite seat next to the chapel, she stopped me and said, "Father, look at these."

Opening her pocketbook, she fished out two pictures. The first photo showed her sitting on that same bench, wearing that same dress, and displaying that same relaxed posture that I saw before me now. The second picture was identical to the first. It all seemed like the twilight zone.

"Like them?" she asked.

"With all my heart," I said, trying not to laugh.

"Here," she said, holding out the pictures. "Pick the one ya like best."

"Am I on Candid Camera?" I wondered to myself.

"Can't ya decide, Father?"

Looking around for hidden cameras, I answered, "I want the real one."

"Which one's that?"

"You!" I said, kissing her forehead.

Blushing, she responded, "But ya can't take me everywhere with ya so take one of my pictures; better yet take both of them. Give one to yer mother."

"Gee whiz, Angie, thanks!" I said, still amused at the look-alike pictures resembling her true presence before me.

"Welcome," she said, smiling proudly.

Once a week, I would order out for a small pizza. On that day I would hear from Angie, "Friday, pizza day! Right, Father?" She always took five slices and I got three. I didn't mind, though; the real treat for me was seeing her enjoy herself. With a satisfactory belch at the end of her feast, Angie would always then tap her round belly with both hands, wrap her firm arms around me, and say, "Thanks Father. 'Cuz of ya, there's more of me. Next Friday, pizza day! Right?"

"Bet your life!" I said.

Some months later, as I knelt on a kneeler in the viewing room, praying privately for Dolores, a deceased resident, I noticed Angie behind me. Leaning over the casket, she commented, "Father, will ya look at that hairdo and gold earrings! Don't they match her glasses? My, my, what a gorgeous gown! And the makeup—out of this world! Such beauty! Don't ya think?"

I nodded in agreement.

"I hope they can make me look half as beautiful when my time comes," she continued. "Father, who is she anyway?"

"Who is she?" I laugh. "You know her."

"I do?"

"That's Dolores."

"That's Dolores? I didn't even know she was dead. Wow! She looks better off. O my! I pray I look like her, instead of an old goat, when my time comes," she said, patting her hair.

The next day, running late for Dolores' funeral Mass, I hurried into chapel.

"Psst!" Angie spoke around her index finger. "I wanna see ya."

"Not now, Angie. I'm late for Mass."

"No you're not," she said in an audible whisper, "It didn't start yet."

"Funny." I said. Leaning towards her, I asked, "Well, what is it?"

"Come here!" she demanded. Climbing over a few pew people, I made quite a distraction among the mourners. Finally, I reached Angie.

"Shh," she said, handing me some *Cheetos*. "Don't tell anybody."

Taking the bright orange, crunchy snacks, I smiled at everyone looking at me. "OK, it's our secret." From whom I didn't know. "Thanks, Angie. Because of you there will be more of me," I said. "No eating in church now. Keep the hour-fast."

Cracking a smile, she responded, "I will, Father, I promise."

Later, at communion time, Angie winked at me.

"Body of Christ," I said.

"Amen," she responded, sticking out her bright orange tongue!

On other occasions, I noticed that Angie often held her fist closed. "Is your arthritis acting up?" I would ask her.

"O no, Father. I ain't got arthritis." She opened up her hand,

and I saw that small plastic angel with the wings folded down. "It's Little Jeanne, my guardian angel. I go ta bed like this," she said. She closed her grip around the angel's image and placed her clenched fist upon her heart. "After a good night sleep my angel wakes me up by pinching my back. She reminds me that I have another day ta git ready for my wedding banquet with my King Bridegroom."

"But don't you say your morning prayers?"

"Yeah, I pray, 'Angel of God, my guardian dear, to whom God's love commits me here, ever this day be at my side, to light, to guard, to rule and guide. Amen.'"

"My, you're really devoted to your angel."

"I better be, 'cuz no one else will be if I don't be. We're all devoted to the Blessed Mother, Blessed Jeanne Jugan, and all the saints, but no one is devoted to my Little Jeanne, but me. Besides, my angel is devoted to me, too. I keep her busy, just for me, to ask Jesus to make me His beautiful Queen Bride. Tomorrow, pizza day! Right?"

"You betcha!"

The following year, Angie began to lose touch with reality. No more pizza days—how I missed them!

One particular Thursday, Angie asked Sister Amez if she could get her hair done, because she said she was going out on Friday. Sister called her daughter to see if someone was coming to take her out. Her daughter said that no one was taking her out. However, Angie still insisted that she was going out on Friday. Anyway, that Thursday, she went down to Ellie, the hairdresser, to have her hair done. The beautician told me later the divine story about her:

"As she sat under the hair dryer, she spoke to me about how

handsome and divine her bridegroom appeared. Standing up, Angie said, 'O my, here He comes again. I gotta go!'

'Where,' I asked, 'and who's coming?'

'My bridegroom is here. Can't you see Him?' she asked, walking away from me with her face all aglow and her hair still damp."

On Friday, Angie came to the dinner table all dolled up. With her hair done beautifully, she wore a string of fake pearls around her neck. Her earrings matched her silver glasses. Her fragrant perfume filled the air. In her hand, she squeezed her Little Jeanne.

Suddenly, toward the end of the meal, she began choking. Sister Amez and the nurses came running and did everything possible to save her. Quickly, I anointed her. Angie turned purple and died lying on the floor, clutching her Little Jeanne. Our roly-poly Angie had boarded heaven's bus—on schedule as planned—for her wedding banquet. Unlike me, she was ready and unafraid.

Later that day, I met Sister Amez again, and repeated her earlier advice to me, "You never know. He may come like a 'thief in the night'."

"I know;" she responded wisely, "at a time you least expect Him."

In the casket, Angie's body appeared in radiant beauty—her silver hair done up better than ever, her dress in a silvery gown, sparkling silver earrings, fragrant perfume, out-of-this-world makeup, and her diamond-like rosary glittered around her left hand with her Little Jeanne angel clutched in her right hand over her heart. Abby, the funeral directress, had made her body look more beautiful than Dolores could have imagined. Her prayer had been answered. No more seeing herself as an old goat, our Angie

Angel, now feasts, I do believe, at the eternal pizzeria of the King Bridegroom as His beautiful *Queen Bride*.

> **As a young man marries a virgin,**
> **Your Builder shall marry you,**
> **And as a bridegroom rejoices in his bride**
> **So shall your God rejoice in you.**

—Isaiah 62:5

ETTY

The Beautiful Hands of the Priest

Early one afternoon, during a bingo game in our social hall, the beepers blasted. Distracted from her game, Betty asked, "Is someone dying?"

"Yes, it's Rose," I said.

"O, Father Christopher, can I come and pray for her?"

"Sure, but call me Father Chris; I must hurry!"

"Go ahead," she said. "I'll meet you there."

Entering Rose's room, I saw the little altar with the crucifix between two burning candles that the Little Sisters set up when someone is dying. They take turns praying at the bedside for the dying resident. It's called the *"Watch"*, a most holy time and the climax of their sacred ministry. These Little Sisters are the midwives of Christ, I always say, because they help the Divine Physician deliver souls to their eternal birthdays.

Mother Vincent, on this *"Watch,"* handed me a stole, the ritual for the dying, and holy water. In the midst of the Little Sisters, I began the *Rite For The Dying*. After I anointed her with all the blessings of the Church, we 'watched' for the Divine Deliverer to come and take our Rose home to the glorious garden in heaven.

During our prayerful silence, Rose's only son rushed into the room, pushed us out of the way, and kissed his mother. He stood next to her the whole time, rubbing his fingers through her hair. As he caressed her, Betty entered the room. Sitting down, she thumbed her beads. After praying the rosary, she shook her head back and forth, like a Ping-Pong ball in play.

Suddenly, Rose took two quick breaths and breathed no more. In the sight of all, except for Betty, it was a blessed death. Sister Amez whispered, "Our Rose now blooms in paradise." And referring to one of Blessed Jeanne Jugan's sayings, she added, "God wanted her for Himself."

The next day, I joined Sister Amez and some of the residents sitting on the patio above the garden. We were speaking about our beloved Rose when Betty asked, "Father Chris, who was that man with his hands on her head when she was dying, the doctor?"

"That was her son," Sister Amez answered.

"Well, when my time comes, Father, I wish for your hands to be on my head and not any of my children."

"Why Father's?" a resident asked.

"Because," she proclaimed, "his hands are anointed. The hands of Father Chris are the hands of the Lord; his beautiful hands give us the body and blood of Christ."

"Betty, where did you get your priestly wisdom?" I asked. "From my sermons?"

"No, of course not, Father. It was Jesus who told me in a dream that your hands are His." I was humbled and exalted. Lowering her voice to a whisper, she said, "Father, please, when I'm dying move all my kids out of the way and lay your hands on my head to make my only wish come true." She took my hands in hers. "Do it like this," she said, lifting my hands upon her head.

"Now that feels good." She kissed my palms. "O my, what beautiful hands you have!"

Following Betty into the chapel, I led her into the confessional. Being curious, I said, "Please, tell me that dream of yours."

"Sure, Father Chris." Her voice took on a calm and reverent tone. "Well, after praying a 'Hail Mary', a 'Glory Be' and invoking the Holy Spirit, I fell asleep in our chapel. Then I had this dream:

I was a child again, sitting on a boat with my guardian angel. When he faded away, Jesus appeared wearing white Mass vestments. Side-by-side we stood in the warmth of the glittering sun. Like sparkling diamonds, a stream of sunbeams danced on the surface of the dazzling waves. Smacking my lips, I tasted the spray of holy water.

Distracted by a jumping sunfish, the divine fisherman reached overboard and caught it. With the fish flopping in His beautiful hands, He spoke my name, saying, 'Betty, I love you!'

His gaze penetrated my whole being. 'Are you hungry?' He asked me, cupping the little sea creature in His beautiful hands.

Gulping air, the fish stared at me. I told Him, 'No, I'm not. Thanks anyway, Lord, but I have no appetite.' How could the Lord of Life want me to eat His loyal fish, I wondered?

Raising the dying fish to His lips, He said, 'Sorry, your hour has not yet come.' He tossed it back into the life-giving water. As I watched the sunfish flapping under the blue sea, the glorious Lord cupped my face with His radiating hands. They were more brilliant than all the sunbeams.

'O my, what beautiful hands You have!' I said.

'These,' He proclaimed, lifting them before my eyes, 'are the hands of my priests.'

"So, Father Chris, that's how I know your hands are His."

"I see."

"There's more to my dream."

"Go on, please."

"Jesus asked again, 'Are you hungry yet, Betty?'

'I'm starving!' I said.

'Come, eat your meal. Everything is ready.' He walked to the back of the boat, and I followed Him. I thought He was going to catch that graceful fish again; instead, we sat at table. He took bread, broke it, cupped it, and said, 'Take this and eat it.' Taking the Bread of Life from His beautiful hands, I bowed and ate. He disappeared. Feeling alone and afraid about being lost at sea, I cried out,

'Where are You, Lord?'

'Here I am!"

'Where?' I asked, looking all around.

'Here, within your heart,' He whispered and my dream ended.

"Wow, Betty, I wish I could dream like that!"

"And I wish I had your beautiful hands, O my!"

Later that day, I found this poem in my mail box:

THE BEAUTIFUL HANDS OF A PRIEST

We need them in life's early morning,
We need them again at its close;
We feel their warm clasp of true friendship,
We seek them when tasting life's woes.
At the altar each day we behold them,
And the hands of a king on his throne
Are not equal to them in their greatness;
Their dignity stands all alone;
And when we are tempted and wander,
To the pathways of shame and of sin,
It's the hand of a priest that will absolve us —
Not once, but again and again.
And when we are taking life's partner,
Other hands may prepare us a feast,
But the hand that will bless and unite us —
Is the beautiful hand of a priest.
God bless them and keep them all holy
For the Host which their fingers caress;
When can a poor sinner do better,
Than to ask Him to guide thee and bless?
When the hour of death comes upon us,
May our courage and strength be increased,
By seeing raised over us in blessing —
The beautiful hands of a priest.

Soon, Betty's *hour* had come. There was no "Watch", no Little Sisters, no nurse, no residents, and none of her children were present. She didn't feel well that day, so I made a routine visit that night. At her bedside, I saw her gulping air, *like a fish out of water.*

Pushing the emergency button, I called for the nurse. Death was coming "like a thief in the night." After laying my hands on her head, I anointed her. Gazing into the distance—as if seeing someone—she smiled, closed her eyes, and stopped breathing. Right before the nurse arrived, I placed my hands back on her head and kissed her face. Startling me, she exhaled two last breaths as if blowing out a birthday candle.

Still, her angelic face, couldn't calm my nervous spirit. I wondered if I really wanted this ministry to the elderly. I thought that too often I would be in mourning, facing death, that 'Grim Reaper', and the fear of it. But on this particular night, however, I realized that Betty's wish had come true—upon her head were *"the beautiful hands of a priest."*

How is it that such miraculous deeds are accomplished by his hands?

—Mark 6:2

CHRISTINE
His Achilles' Heel

Several days before beginning my assignment at Holy Family Home, I first met Sister Christine who sat in her electric wheelchair at the front desk, selling chances and counting money. Interrupting her, I said, "Excuse me, Sister, please."

"Just a moment," she replied.

"OK, I'll wait."

When she finished counting, she looked up at me.

"Hi! I'm Father Chris, the new chaplain. Can you tell me, Sister, where I can find a cart?" I asked. "I need to move my things in."

Sister sat back in her chair and observed, "So, you're one of those priests."

"I am?"

"Just look at you ... Sneakers, short pants, no collar, and worse of all, a beard."

"These are my work clothes."

"Your work clothes, Father, are black."

In silence, I stood before Sister Christine, like Jesus before Pilate.

"Well now," she said, breaking the quiet, "buy some of these chances for the poor, and I'll find you a cart."

From my pocket, I pulled out a 20-dollar bill. "Give me ten dollars worth," I said, wanting to make a generous impression.

"You'll take twenty!" she insisted, snatching the bill away. "Follow me."

Putting her wheelchair in gear, she ran over my foot.

"What about my stubs?" I asked, hopping on one foot.

"Ye of little faith," she snickered. "Follow me." She sped into the kitchen like a truck driver behind schedule. When I caught up to her, she said, "There, take that cart." One of the kitchen workers asked if I needed help. "He's no invalid," Sister answered, "He must be 200 pounds and six-feet tall."

"I'm 220 and 6' 2," I said, flexing my muscles and making two fists at Sister (behind her back, of course.)

Turning around, she commanded, "Stop wasting time. Take the cart and get to work!"

"Yes, Sister. Thank you, Sister."

"One more thing."

"Yes, Sister?"

"Shave!"

"But, but …"

"No buts. You're the Lord's representative," she said. "You look silly with your red beard and brown hair. I can see that your brown eyes look confused as to what color to be … Father, sheer the beard, wear the collar, and look the part."

"I'll wear the collar, but the beard stays," I insisted.

Grinning, she simply replied, "We'll see."

The next week, in my priestly garb, before meeting with the Sisters that day to begin my new assignment, I met Sister Christine again in her power-chair outside the chapel looking out the door. Seeing my reflection in the glass, she turned around and said, "Come over here, and let me see you." She looked me over from top to bottom. "You've still got the beard."

Saluting her, I said, "I know. I like it. Besides, Jesus had one, too."

"And so did Judas; Father, so did Judas."

Sister Amez, overhearing her remarks, took me aside, saying, "I like your beard. Keep it. Pay no attention to her."

"But she's a drill sergeant," I whined.

Laughing, she said, "You'll get use to her. She has a heart of gold. Wait and see, Father. She's all right."

Throughout the coming week, Sister Christine hounded me until I finally gave in and shaved. Seeing my bare face at last, she proudly proclaimed, "Now, Father Christopher, you look like a priest."

"You can call me Father Chris; I like it better."

"Well, I don't like it better, Father Christopher," she said. Reaching into the bag hanging over the back of her wheelchair, she pulled out three gifts for me: a small plaque of Blessed Jeanne Jugan, a rosary, and a little silver statue of Saint Joseph.

"Thank you, Sister, but you keep the plaque. I already have one."

"Good," she said. "But take the ruby rosary; it's just like mine. I've been praying for you. And take the little silver statue of Saint Joseph to protect you. Keep them in your pocket, like we do, for special graces."

Receiving her gifts, I replied, "I'll pray my first new rosary for your special intention, and I'll keep Saint Joseph at my finger tips."

"No need to pray for my special intention;" she chuckled, "it's already been granted. Feel your face."

Seeing her joy, I asked, "Do you always get what you pray for?"

"Yes, when I pray long enough."

"Well, what's your secret?"

"It's not a secret; I just told you," she said. "Don't you know the parables on praying always and never losing heart?"

"Hey, I'm a priest, remember?"

"I remember, and don't you ever forget it. Our divine Lord has revealed to us that God has an Achilles' heel."

"God has a weakness?" I asked, "But that's poor theology."

"It's rich theology," she retorted.

"And what then, Sister Christine, might His weakness be?"

"It lies in our asking, begging, and pestering Him for what we really want." she answered, "He'll always fulfill our deepest desires as long as we pray long enough and never lose heart. Because of His precious love for beggars, it always works. It's the gospel truth, Father Christopher. Feel your face."

Rubbing my naked cheeks with both hands, I had to wonder.

Before her retirement, Sister Christine was the "Beggar" for the home and one of the best in the order of the Little Sisters of the Poor. At the dock markets, the workers would watch for her.

"Shh, here she comes," the lookout man would say, "Watch the language!"

As if she owned the market, Sister would walk down the long aisles pointing out to the workers the crates of food that were needed.

"I want that, that, and that!" Cases of vegetables and fruits were loaded onto the Holy Family truck. On her charity trips, she always gave out inexpensive holy cards, scapulars, medals, angel pins, rosaries, and images of Blessed Jeanne Jugan from her cigar box.

"They're already blessed by the priest," she would say. "You don't have to make a donation now, but you can if you like. And the sooner the better."

One day in a department store, she picked up some items for some poor residents. The store manager asked her, "Is this cash or charge?"

"Neither," she replied. "It's charity. Bag it!" He then received a blessed rosary, too. "Keep the change," she told him.

After her retirement, Sister received her power-chair. It took her a month to learn how to control it. She almost demolished the building. It may be a coincidence, but that same year (I was told) contractors remodeled Holy Family Home, especially the convent. Mother Superior said of her, "No one deserves the electric chair more than Sister Christine." The comment was made, I think, because of Sister's successful fund-raising.

Toward the end of her prolonged sickness, Sister requested the Sacrament of the Sick. "Father *Chris*," she said, "I need your priesthood, please anoint me. I can't bear this any longer."

"O, so it's Father Chris now, is it?"

"Yes, everyone else calls you, Father Chris, so I may as well, too," she said. "Now I beg you to anoint me." Quoting her foundress, she added, "God wants me for Himself."

"OK," I said. "But we want you for ourselves, too. I'll anoint you, but don't you die on me." We blessed ourselves, and I laid my hands on her bowed head for a silent moment. Dipping my thumb into the sacred oil, I traced the sign of the cross on her forehead, praying, "Through this holy anointing may the Lord in His love and mercy help you with the grace of the Holy Spirit."

"Amen," she prayed.

Dipping my thumb in the oil again, I traced the cross on the palms of her hands, saying, "May the Lord who frees you from sin save you and raise you up."

"Amen," she prayed.

Continuing my prayers, I blessed her with my little Saint

Joseph statue and said, "By the power the Apostolic See has given me, I grant you a plenary indulgence and a pardon for all your sins, in the name of the Father, and of the Son, and of the Holy Spirit."

"Amen," she prayed. "Now, Master, you can let your Little Sister go in peace with Blessed Jeanne Jugan." She referred to the last words of her foundress for herself: "Please, Lord, I have refused You nothing, so open Your gates today for me… I long to see you." Looking in my eyes, she continued, "Beg the Good Lord, Father Chris, for me to die alone, so I can go home with him forever. And the sooner the better." She continued in the words of her foundress: "Let's us love Him very much; that is all that is necessary. He is so good. Do everything through love."

Filled with sadness, I didn't pray for her request. I couldn't let her go yet. That night, however, she told Sister Amez to go to bed.

"I'm all right," she said. Alone, in the early hours of that morning, while holding fast to her ruby rosary, just like mine, Sister Christine met the Saving Lord, and I'm sure she heard His divine proclamation: "Well done, good and faithful servant. Come now, my beloved Christine, and share your master's joy."

Yes, Sister Christine, the benign "drill sergeant" had indeed a golden heart! At the grave, Mother Vincent placed her hand on me. Whispering, she quoted Blessed Jeanne Jugan, "Let's go on for God."

After sprinkling holy water on her casket, we all watched the sacred drops bead off. Seeing my reflection off the gray coffin, I smiled at the thought of our beloved beggar, doing what she did best, begging the Harvest Master for all our needs. Rubbing my shaved face, I figured that God would never deny her pestering prayers for us, and I trusted that she would always have our special intentions answered. After all, she knew, and would know forever, *His Achilles' heel.*

So I say unto you, 'Ask and you shall receive ...'

—Luke 11:9

DOLLY

What a New Life!

Under the weather on this particular day, she sat at the dinner table.

"How's Dolly?" I asked.

"I'm exhausted, Father," she said, sipping her tea. "Last night the nurse woke me and gave me a sleeping pill. After that, for the life of me, I couldn't get back to sleep."

"Ahh, that's too bad. You'll sleep tonight."

"I know I will, if they don't wake me with their sleeping pills."

One day after Mass, the 93-year-old Dolly waited for me outside the chapel, saying, "Father Chris, I got cancer. I'm afraid." She cried, and I fought back my tears. "Please, give me your blessing."

Rubbing her arm, I said, "Sure, let's go back in chapel." In the sanctuary, we stood before the tabernacle. Taking my holy oils from my pocket, I anointed her.

"Now, I feel better," she said.

The next time I saw Dolly, she asked, "Can we talk? I'm afraid again."

"OK, let's go to your room."

Arriving there, I admired the cross hanging on her wall. It

depicted the Risen Christ.

"Dolly, we can conquer all things in Him—even the grave," I said, looking at the victorious Jesus. "Trust Him, keep praying, and it will be Alleluia time!"

"Keep talking, Father, you're getting through," she said, gazing up at her crucifix.

At that moment, a personal story of death and resurrection came to mind. "Do you know about the Pink Sisters on Green Street?" I asked, referring to the Holy Spirit Adoration Sisters, a cloistered order of nuns who perpetually adored the Lord in His Most Blessed Sacrament.

"Certainly, I do. I used to go there to adore our Blessed Lord, surrounded by all the carved angels above," she said. "You hear their confessions, right?"

"That's right," I said. "Anyway, a few weeks ago one of the sisters gave me a gift. It was a see-through container with a screen on top of it. A caterpillar in its cocoon hung by a thread.

'Be careful driving home, watch out for the bumps,' Sister told me, 'and go easy on the turns. In a week or so, you'll see a miracle of nature.'

'I will?'

'You sure will.'

'Sister, are you trying for an easy penance?'

'It's fragile, Father, so handle it with prayer,' the nun said."

"Dolly, when I arrived back home, I placed the container on my desk. Each morning, I woke and looked at the hanging cocoon. Nothing seemed to be happening. After a week, I thought it was dead, and that I should get rid of it, but Sister Amez convinced me to keep it for one more day, saying, 'It will be the 8th day.'"

"And what happened on the 8th day?" Dolly asked. "Did you get rid of it?"

"No! Upon waking, I looked into the container, and behold, I saw—looking at me—a beautiful monarch butterfly spreading its glorious wings; it was orange with black designer lines all through it. I gasped! Then, I checked my door to make sure it was locked. Did Sister Amez come in during the night, I wondered, and place that beautiful creature into the container? Dolly, it was incredible!"

"O Father, what a story!"

"There's more, Dolly. The next day, when its wings were dryer, Sister Amez and I took the container to the garden. Lifting off the screen, she put her hand inside. The transformed creature plopped onto her index finger and slowly flapped its wings. After a while, she lifted it high. Taking a last look at her, it flew into the blue.

'It is risen!' Sister proclaimed. 'And we, too, shall rise.'

'Alleluia!' I responded. Fluttering down, it landed on one of the flowers and sucked nectar—no more eating dirt and taking forever to go anywhere. What a miracle of nature!'"

"And what a new life!" Dolly exclaimed.

A few days later, I saw her again. She sat all alone crying on the bench outside the front doors.

"O Father Chris, I'm afraid again."

Taking her hand, I said, "Dolly, today, I'm not going to talk to you; instead, I'm going to let Jesus talk to you." Spreading out my flapping arms, like a butterfly, I landed my hands on her sweet head, silently placing His priesthood upon her and hoping that the Risen Lord would transform her fears and mine.

Breaking the sacred quiet, she said, "O Father, I feel better. Where would we be without the priest." She sniffled. "I'm dying inside the cocoon of my body, but I don't mind. The Risen Lord will transform me like he did that butterfly, only more beautiful," she said, placing her hand over her precious heart.

*Silence **is** golden!* I thought.

On a Sunday shortly thereafter, Dolly and another resident brought up the offertory gifts for Mass. Both of them limped up the aisle, but Dolly grabbed the back of each pew holding on for dear life. They seemed like caterpillars taking forever to get to me. Yet, my heart was touched. They were so proud. Smiling, I received the gifts, saying, "Good job!" They beamed. The next day as I was rushing to the chapel, Dolly intercepted me.

"Father, can I see you after Mass?"

O no, I thought. I felt impatient this time and felt bad about it. Thinking she wanted me to pray over her again, I said, "Let's do it now; I won't have time after Mass."

"Good, let's sit down," she said.

"Fine," I said, impatiently.

"Father, I wanted you to know that when I brought up the gifts yesterday."

"Yes, Dolly," I said, interrupting her.

"And you took them from me—"

"Right," I said, continuing my arrogance.

"Well, I didn't see you, Father,"

"Then, Dolly, who?"

"I saw Jesus," she said, bowing her head as she humbled me real good.

"Dolly, I'm glad you told me this. Now I'll celebrate the Mass better than ever."

She smiled. I helped her up, and together we entered the chapel in slow motion—like two *caterpillars*. This time Dolly ministered to me, His impatient priest. Now, I felt better.

A few weeks later, Dolly was confined to bed; Sister Amez was brushing Dolly's pure white hair as I entered the room. Believing that she wouldn't live out the day, Sister said, "Father, Dolly is expecting a special visitor today. Isn't that right, honey?"

"Yes, Sister," she moaned.

"Tell Father who's coming."

"O, he knows," she said. "And you know what, Father?"

"What, Dolly?"

"I'm not afraid anymore."

"Alleluia!" I said, spreading out my fluttering hands, wishing I had no fear of death, like her.

"Please, Father, my last rites."

After anointing her, I blessed her with the plenary indulgence of the Church and ended with the prayers for the dying.

"Now, I'm ready," she groaned, "to break out of my cocoon."

"That's the spirit!" I said. "Dolly, I'm going to the Pink Sisters, but I'll be back soon."

"Good, Father. Ask that Sister who gave you the dying caterpillar to pray for me that I break out of this old cocoon," she said, moaning with her hands crossed over her heart.

"It will be her penance," I said.

Returning home that evening, while everyone was still eating supper, I hurried straight to tell Dolly that all the Pink Sisters were praying their penance for her. Knocking, I said, "Dolly, it's me."

Slowly, opening the door, I saw her stripped bed, and a shiver charged up my spine. I knew she had emerged from the cocoon of her body. Beside her empty bed, I knelt and prayed,

"Eternal rest grant to Dolly, O Lord…."

Standing up, I thought about that butterfly. As I turned around, Sister Amez walked in. "Father, Dolly left this world fearless and wide-awake," she said. "Right before she died, she had that long gaze, staring into the corner of the room as if seeing someone."

"Maybe she was looking at her special visitor."

"Perhaps, but also, there was a flowery fragrance coming off her body and a golden aura surrounding her countenance. Then, she took her last breaths to take her place, I believe, with Him in heaven. What a blessed death!"

"And," I exclaimed, *"what a new life!"*

I am the Resurrection and the life,
whoever believes in me ... will never die.

—John 11:25

ELLIE

Eucharistic Serenader

"Sleep now ... shh," she whispered. Ellie rocked back and forth in her chair. Stroking her stuffed lamb, she continued, "Shh, shh, go to sleep, Lammy, you had a rough day."

Eating some apple slices out of a cup, I walked into the room and offered her one. Looking at me, she squinted at my collar.

"Amen," she said, sticking out her tongue. I placed an apple slice on it. Closing her eyes, she blessed herself. After savoring the fruit, she said, "O Father, I thought you were giving me communion. Mmm! Give me another."

"One for Lammy, too?"

"No, he's sleeping now. Besides, he never eats. Give me his."

"Here, take them all."

Grabbing the cup, she said, "Yummy, how sweet the taste! You know we need the priest to wake us up and tell us we belong to God."

Poking the stuffed lamb, I said, "Wake up, Lammy, you belong to God."

"Not, Lammy, Father. He already knows. Shh, shh, go back to sleep, sweet heart."

On another visit, I anointed Ellie. In her sick bed, she hugged her stuffed lamb. After the prayers, she said, "Maybe I'll go to heaven now. And, if I do, I'm bringing Lammy with me. Do you know, Father, that when I woke this morning, he was hugging me. He's so good! It's been two years now, and I haven't had to give him even a glass of water. Never a bit of trouble. What an angel!"

"He's that good?"

"Yep, he is!"

"Well, why not leave him here with us when you go to heaven? Then he can help us be good, like you."

"No way! There're too many clowns around here. He goes with me and that's it!" she shouted. "Now, lay your hands on him, Father, and make him ready, like me, for heaven, because you got the power."

Laying my hands on her stuffed pet, I said, "God bless you and Lammy." In my own heart, I prayed, "Make me ready, O Lord, like Ellie, for heaven."

Barely able to walk, Ellie would shuffle her feet down the stairwell to perform her daily ritual. Leaning on the walls, she would go to the chapel, praying all the way there, "O my God, O my God, O my God." It seemed that the Eucharistic Lord was drawing her every day to visit him. Holding onto the pews, she would struggle her way up the middle aisle before the altar. After a profound bow, she would take a good long look at the bigger-than-life-size crucifix in the sanctuary. Then she would sit down in the first pew and gaze at the tabernacle, for at least an hour, totally absorbed in His Real Presence.

For Ellie's birthday I offered Mass for her intentions. At the sign of peace, I left the altar to extend my birthday greetings. As I reached out my hand, she stuck out her tongue. "Happy 95th Birthday!" I said, kissing her on the forehead.

"Where's Jesus?" she asked.

"On the altar," I said.

"Then go git 'im!"

"OK, I'll be back."

"Wonderful!" she exclaimed.

Bringing her Holy Communion, I said, "Body of Christ."

"It's about time," she responded, sticking out her tongue. When she buried her face in her hands to be alone with the Lord, I'd noticed a new watch on her wrist. I wondered who would give her that gift since she couldn't even tell time. She lived only in the eternal now.

The next day was Palm Sunday, one I'll never forget. Mother Vincent, Sister Amez and I proclaimed the Passion of Christ that included the three denials of Peter. Ending my homily, I pointed to the crucifix above the altar, saying, "Lord Jesus crucified, have mercy on us."

As I left the pulpit and bowed before the altar, Ellie's watch suddenly crowed out the 11 o'clock hour. Eleven times we heard the sound effects of *Cock-a-doodle-doo*. Mindful of my sins, I knelt and beat my breast 11 times, praying, "Lord Jesus crucified, have mercy on me." Afterwards, I stood, turned to the congregation, and asked, "For whom the cock crows? It crows for thee and me."

Ellie's eyes were focused on the crucifix above. I wondered if she had heard a word I said. What made this story even more mysterious was that the sound effects of the cock crowing occurred not on the hour, at 11 o'clock, but rather 11:15, immediately after the closing words of my homily: "Lord Jesus crucified, have mercy on us."

Is that odd," I thought, "or is that God?" I quickly learned there are no coincidences only God incidences.

On my first Good Friday at Holy Family Home, I felt anxious over the service. Since my mother and father would be in the congregation, I wanted to be at my best for the ones who first intro-duced me to the Crucified One. Adding to my nervousness, my parents took their seats in the first pew, right in front of the pulpit.

"O my God, O my God, O my God," my heart whispered, "come to my assistance."

It was bad enough that Mom and Dad would be sitting in front during my preaching, but what made it worse—they were sitting in Ellie's seat!

"Lord, make haste to help me!" I prayed.

Silently processing down the middle aisle, I passed my parents. Not seeing Ellie, I prostrated before the stripped altar. Relieved by her absence, I thought that maybe she fell asleep with Lammy. Perhaps, she won't make it today, I hoped in the silence of Good Friday. After the narration of the Passion, I began my homily quoting from the first reading, Isaiah 53:5,

"But he was pierced for our offenses, crushed for our sins . . . " Pointing up at the crucifix above the altar, I continued, "Behold the Lamb of God who was pierced ..."

"O my God, O my God, O my God..."

Suddenly, Ellie made her appearance, shuffling all the way down the center aisle to the foot of the altar where she bowed and took a good long look up at the huge crucifix. Then, climbing over my father, she sat next to my mother. Stretching her neck up like a telescope, she squinted over the altar into the emptied taber-nacle. I feared she would cry out, "Where's Jesus!" She didn't, thank God.

Somewhat relieved, I picked up where I left off, "Behold the Lamb of God who was pierced for our offenses, and crushed for our sins ..."

"O my, I can't stand this!" Ellie suddenly exclaimed, elbowing my mother. Standing up between my parents, she started singing,

"O Sacrament Most Holy, O Sacrament Divine, all praise and all thanksgiving be every moment Thine."

Sister Amez rushed down the aisle with a wheelchair to rescue my preaching from our sacramental singing resident. Like a queen on a mobile throne, Ellie serenaded our absent Eucharistic King, echoing the hymn throughout the whole chapel:

> *O Lord I am not worthy*
> *That thou should come to me,*
> *But speak the words of comfort*
> *My spirit healed shall be.*
> *And humbly I'll receive Thee*
> *The Bridegroom of my soul*
> *No more by sin to grieve Thee*
> *Or fly Thy sweet control....*

As Ellie's melodious voice faded, I shortened my homily:

"Though he was harshly treated, he submitted and opened not his mouth; like a lamb led to slaughter or a sheep before the shearers, he was silent and opened not his mouth" (Isaiah 53:7). Gazing up at the crucifix, I ended my twice-interrupted, shortened Good Friday homily, saying, "Take a good long look at the Crucified One, and Behold the Lamb of God!"

On Ascension Thursday morning, Ellie suddenly passed away in her sleep while hugging Lammy. The funeral director had to pry her stuffed pet from her clutched hands. Her serene face wore a child's grin. You never know, I thought, He may be coming for me soon.

At her viewing, I knelt in front of the opened casket and saw her stuffed lamb cuddled at the right side of her body. After petting

Lammy, I caressed the silver corpus on her sapphire rosary, wrapped around her hands. I took a good long look at the Lamb of God on it. Focused on her rosary crucifix, I whispered a prayer:

"Crucified One, pierced for our offenses and crushed for our sins, dispel my fear of death, like you did for your *Eucharistic Serenader*."

Let the children come to me.

—Matthew 19:14

FREDDY
A Soaring Eagle

Calmly, Freddy sat rocking in his room, praying the rosary, and watching the Eagles game. As I entered, he said, "Father Chris, turn that dumb thing off."

"Turn off the Eagles?" I felt his forehead. "I heard you've been sick."

"Father," he whispered, "I was right there!"

"Right where?"

"At the pearly gates. And He was surrounded by angels!" Freddy's face beamed.

"Who was?"

"I really saw him."

"Jesus?"

"For sure!"

"What did He look like?"

"Brilliantly beautiful," he said. "His deep brown eyes shone upon me; I could barely see. He radiated my whole being. It was awesome, I tell ya, awesome!"

"Go on, please."

"I'll start from the beginning:"

After praying my rosary, I saw myself, as a boy, walking on puffy-pink-clouds. Heavenly, it was. Being outside the gates of paradise, I looked for Saint Peter, but instead, I saw Jesus in all His majesty with His angels embracing trumpets. He wore golden vestments and a gold wristwatch. Hoping He would open the gates, I waited in His glorious gaze. Then, He smiled, and the angels lipped their trumpets. Lifting up His blue sleeve, He looked at His watch, saying, 'Freddy, Fred ...'

"Waking up, I felt the nurse poking me. Angry that I didn't get inside the celestial gates, I poked her right back, twice. Father, I'm really looking forward to heaven. Christ the King—He's the greatest!"

"Wow!" I exclaimed. "I wish I could dream like you."

"Dream? That was no dream; Father, it was the real McCoy. I haven't been the same ever since. I don't even care if the Eagles win or lose. I only care about going through those pearly gates and making a touchdown in the kingdom of God. Then he added, "Father, I need a confession."

"OK, what are your sins?"

"I poked a nurse twice."

"And she deserved it," I said.

"Father, you need a confession, too."

"I know, Freddy, but for your penance, pray the 'Hail Mary' twice for the poking nurse."

"And I'll pray three for you, Father Chris."

After the absolution, he looked intensely at his watch, asking, "When do you think He's coming for me?"

"Who knows," I said. "Be patient, like me, and wait your turn."

"You gotta be patient. You're young, but I'm old and can't wait."

"You'll wait," I said, turning the Eagles' back on. "Who's the best Eagle of all time?" I asked.

"Concrete Charlie, of course, the last of the 60–minute men. Did you know, Father, he prays the rosary everyday?"

"No, I didn't, Freddy, but I do know he's not the best Eagle of all time. And you better not tell Chuck Bednarek; he'll beat us up."

"I won't tell. I don't even know him, although I read his book, *The Last of the Sixty-Minute Men*. But who do you say is the best Eagle, Father?"

"Saint John, the Beloved disciple, of course. No one soars like him, not even the birds, except maybe you. You should have been called John."

"That's my Confirmation name."

"Hey, I figured there was a connection. OK, so long, Freddy, and keep soaring."

"You, too, Father."

"I wish I could."

During Advent, I sat with Freddy in the tea room enjoying a cup of hot chocolate. Sipping his drink, he said, "Who's that Ellen think she was anyway dying before me."

"Now, Frederick John, calm down. You know God makes that call. Besides, it's Advent and you've got to wait your turn."

"It's always Advent around here. I've been waiting all year, and it bothers me when someone jumps ahead of the line."

"Fred, it was Ellen's time, not yours."

"But I'm older."

"How old?"

"Too old to remember."

"Well, a little bird told me you're 99."

"Then, it's high time I fly across His goal line."

"Don't you want another year of life? Not many people live to be 100, you know. Think of it… I'll call *Action News*. When they ask your secret for longevity, you can tell them it's the humble chaplain here."

Laughing, he responded, "Keep *Action News* away; I'd rather have you call Abby, my undertaker. She's the last to let you down, you know?"

"Really?"

"Yeah, but only in a *grave* situation," he kidded. "She carries out everything she undertakes. I hope someone calls her soon to come for my body because I'm Ready Freddy."

Chuckling, I answered, "But heaven's not ready for Freddy, so let's change the subject."

"Let's not, Father, because I can't wait." He looked at his watch. "When is He coming for me?"

"Next Advent, I hope. Just imagine your party in heaven after living 100 years on earth."

"Party? I'm tired of parties." He frowned. "I just wanna go home to the Lord and soon, very soon."

The following year, we celebrated Freddy's 100th birthday with Mass and a surprise party in the social hall. There, he received a football gift signed by all the Eagle players. The signature he treasured the most was the one I signed: *Saint John, the Best Soaring Eagle.*

That evening, I stopped at his room and gave him a good night blessing. He sat holding his prized football, surrounded by all his birthday gifts. Laying my hands on him, I said a thanksgiving prayer for all the years of his precious life. After the blessing, he asked, "Do you know my most precious gift?"

"Your football?"

"No, the Holy Eucharist!" he proclaimed. "Now, I'm ready to soar across the pearly goal line." Spiking the football onto the tile floor, he raised his arms up in triumph and smiled.

Picking up the ball, I pitched it to him, saying, "Go, Freddy, go!"

Before his "winning touchdown" into the kingdom of God, Freddy shared with me one more of his dreams:

After I prayed my rosary and sang to the Holy Ghost, I found myself, as a boy, climbing up a mountain. Following an angel on a grassy path, I saw cows and bears, lions and lambs, cats and birds, and beautiful monarch butterflies.

At the summit stood the beloved disciple. An eagle, perched on the limb, was pecking at an apple. Then, by the swish of his hand, John commanded the king of the birds to fly upward. It flapped its jumbo wings and flew into the sky, parting the white cloud above us. Out of the cloud appeared the pearly gates and the King of Glory, with His angels and their ready trumpets. As He looked at His gold watch, His face radiated and crystallized everything on the mountainside, especially me. Then, He spoke: 'Yes, Frederick John, I Am coming soon—and before Abby—to take you with Me so that where I Am you also may be.'

"Wow! That's quite a dream, Frederick."

"Dream? That was no dream, Father. That's the real McCoy!"

"Anyway, I wish I could soar like you," I said, remembering the attractive Bible with the ascended Lord in the midst of His angelic trumpeters on rose-tinted clouds that I saw on my first day here in the chapel.

"Father, do you think I'm ready for heaven?"

"You betcha!"

That same year, *eight days* after the feast of the Beloved disciple on the feast of the Epiphany of the Lord, Freddy's body was found dead in bed. By his side was his Bible opened to the last page. The holy book was well thumbed, dog-eared, and marked up. His glowing face wore the countenance of victory as Abby and her helpers, Jimmy and Johnny, took his mortal remains away, passing by my gloomy sadness.

For the viewing, his body was dressed in a blue suit, white shirt, and golden tie. His black rosary was wrapped around his hands. His gold watch was on his right wrist. His football sat at the bottom of the casket between his feet. At his side was his old tattered Bible. I picked up his holy book and read the words he had underlined on the last page of the Sacred Scriptures in the Book of Revelation. He had also handwritten his name and Abby's within the text:

"Yes, *(Frederick John)* I am coming soon! *(Before Abby)* Amen! Come, Lord Jesus!"

Along with Saint John, my friend, Ready Freddy, truly was *a soaring eagle.*

For thus says the Lord:
Behold, like an eagle he soars ...

—Jeremiah 48:40

GERTY

Sacred Feet of Jesus

"**H**urry, Fadder, hurry! It's Gerty. I need confession. So hurry, please!" Such was the message I heard on my voice mail one day from our newest resident. Rushing out of my room, I hurried to my new penitent.

"Gerty, how are you?"

"Jest the same, Fadder. I've short breath."

"Me, too," I said, huffing and puffing.

"I also got weak legs, and I'm all tired out."

"Me, too," I said.

With her magnified blue eyes, Gerty looked me over through the thick lenses of her round-golden glasses. Above her bed I saw two framed paintings: the Sacred Heart of Jesus and the Immaculate Heart of Mary. Between them hung an old, rugged crucifix. Looking upon her bureau I saw a little cracked angel and next to it there was a small quartered, broken statue—from the knees down only—upon a pedestal. Looking at the statue, I asked, "What saint is that?"

"O Fadder, that ain't no saint. That's the Sacred Feet of Jesus. It's from His feet that we're lifted up into His heart when we go ta confession." She picked it up, kissed His feet, and gave it to me. "Keep it," she said. "It's blessed and its yers fer comin' ta hear my confession."

Sitting next to Gerty, I began: "In name of the Father, and of the Son, and of the Holy Spirit." She said nothing. "How long since your last confession?"

"Last Saturday."

"OK, what's your sins?"

"Sins? I got no sins. I'm 95. What can I do?"

"Well, have you been impatient, unkind?"

"Na, I mind my business and stay ta myself."

"Do you say your prayers?"

"Everyday I pray my rosary, go ta Mass, receive Holy Communion and pray the Guardian Angel prayer day and night," she said, pointing to her little cracked angel with her white rosary dangling from her hand. "I even got the last rites three times."

"Wonderful, but are you sure you have no sins?"

"Positive!"

"Are you lonely?"

"Is that a sin?"

"Of course not."

"That's good. Ya know, Fadder, yer never as close ta God than when yer alone."

Smiling, I said, "Make your act of contrition."

"You forgot to give my penance?"

"Pray your Guardian Angel prayer," I said, absolving her sinless confession.

"Thanks!" She was trying to remember something. As I was walking out the door, she yelled, "Fadder!"

"Yes?"

"When ya comin' back ta hear my confession again?"

"What fer? Ya got no sins," I said, imitating her.

"What fer? Yer the priest; don't ya know?"

"No, tell me."

"Haven't ya heard the one about the school girl goin' to confession twice in fifteen minutes?"

"No."

"Anyway, the pastor recognized her voice the second time and asked, 'Weren't ya jest in here?'

'Yeah, I was,' the girl said.

'Why are ya back again?'

'Fer more grace, more grace,' the little girl said."

"I knew that," I said. "I'll be back next Saturday for your confession and give you more grace."

"Yeah, that's right. I need all I can git ta rest my weary soul."

"Me, too."

"Thank ya, Fadder, and God bless ya real good!"

Holding the Sacred Feet against my heart, I left her remembering the definition of a sacrament. "A sacrament is an outward sign instituted by Christ **to give grace**." That same day, I, too, received the Sacrament of Reconciliation—for more grace, as well.

The following Saturday we repeated the same routine.

"Gerty, how are you?"

"Jest the same, Fadder; I got short breath, weak legs, and I'm all tired out," she said, holding her dangling rosary.

"Ahh, I'm sorry. So then, what are your sins?"

"Sins? I got no sins. What can I do at my age? I jest want ta rest my weary soul." After I heard her sinless confession again, she asked, "So you'll be back next Saturday for my confession?"

"Of course."

That same month, Gerty became seriously sick. In her room—with death coming closer—we celebrated the Sacrament of Reconciliation again.

"Hi, Gerty?"

"Ya know me?"

"Sure, everyone knows you."

"They do? How?"

"We hear your sweet singing voice in chapel."

"O my," she said.

"Gerty, do you know me?"

She squinted at my collar.

"Yeah."

"What's my name?

"Fadder."

"Father who?"

"Fadder *Christ*," she said, bowing her head.

Being humbled, I asked, "Do you want a confession?"

"Certainly!"

Sitting down next to her, I began, "In the name of the Father, and of the Son, and of the Holy Spirit." Hand-cuffed by her rosary, she blessed herself with both hands and said nothing.

"How long since your last confession?"

"I don't remember."

"What are your sins?"

"I don't remember."

"OK, for your penance pray a Hail Mary. Make the Act of Contrition."

"I don't remember."

After the absolution, she told me she felt better. As I was leaving, she asked, "What's my penance again?"

"I don't remember," I said

"O, I remember," she spurted. "The Guardian Angel prayer."

I kissed her good-bye.

"Now my soul's at rest." she faintly whispered.

After that confession, she hardly spoke; and if she did, she mumbled to herself. For her last months, she just wandered around the home. How I missed her sinless confessions!

One day, I sat next to her in the tea room. All I could see in her was Jesus, beaming through her childlike countenance. Leaning over, she held out to me a jelly pastry. It was slit down the middle. It reminded me of our life size statue of Blessed Jeanne Jugan holding out from her basket a bread roll, also slit down the middle. One would think about the slit open heart of Christ and His sacrificial offering.

"No, thank you, Gerty," I said. "It's almost time for Mass."

Like a silent angel, she just smiled radiantly at me.

A short time later, during the Mass, Gerty shuffled up in line for Holy Communion.

"Body of Christ."

Smiling, in that same holy glow, she handed me that jelly pastry, whispering, "Amen, Father Christ."

Sister Amez, right behind her, received Holy Communion and took the pastry away from her and my sweet Gerty back to her pew. It was such a precious moment that before the end of Mass during the communion meditation, I wondered, could it be that as I was feeding His flock, He was feeding me Himself in a different form of bread? Ending the Mass, I reverenced the altar, and the choir sang out the hymn, *Like A Shepherd*:

> *Like a shepherd, he feeds his flock*
> *And gathers the lambs in his arms,*
> *Holding them carefully close to his heart,*
> *Leading them home.*

Is that odd or is that God? I thought. That's God!

On a Saturday morning in May, Gerty lay dying in her bed, hand-cuffed by her white string-rosary. I was getting out of the shower when the beepers went off, calling us to Gerty's side. By the time, I arrived, Father Steve, a priest visiting his mother, was already ministering the Sacrament of the Sick to our Gerty. After the anointing, she stopped breathing for a long minute and then breathed again. Opening her eyes, she focused on me and spoke clearly: "O Fadder *Christ*, thanks for coming to hear my confession."

Stunned by her words, everyone left me alone with her. Wrapping the purple stole around my neck, and without giving her a penance, I started the absolution prayer. "God the Father of mercies through the death and—"

"But I haven't confessed my sins."

"What sins?"

"Not going to confession for over a year."

"Is that it?"

"That's enough," she said.

"God the Father of mercies—"

"You didn't give me a penance."

"A Hail Mary and the Guardian Angel prayer," I said, "and make the Act of Contrition."

"I already did," she said. "Am I going home soon?"

I mistakenly assumed she thought she was in the hospital, so I placed my hands on hers, saying, "Gerty, you're already home."

"Not yet," she said. "Thank you, Father Christ; now I feel better."

"It's Father Chris, remember?" She just smiled. "I'll let you rest now."

The nurse, the aides, and the Sisters came back into the room and spoke with her. Clearly, she answered the medical questions of how she felt. She looked and spoke better that day than when I first met her. There was a quality presence in her, a spiritual radiance. A half-hour later, when I was attending my other priestly duties, my beeper sounded again. Back in Gerty's room, I gazed upon her body, blessed it, and knew she had gone home to her place in heaven.

A beautiful golden aura, like a halo, shone around her sweet countenance and a fragrance filled the room. Her warm body rested peacefully under the crucifix on the wall and the paintings of the Sacred Heart of Jesus and the Immaculate Heart of Mary. She died humbly beneath the feet of Jesus and Mary. Even though it was a peaceful death, I shuddered at the thought of that 'Grim Reaper'.

Distracting me, Sister Amez said, "He took our angel, just as He promised, to her place in heaven."

"I thought she was getting better." I replied.

"She did get better, Father, and you never know."

Later that day in the art room, I took my broken gift, the one Gerty gave me, and brushed its chipped feet with red paint to depict the sacred wounds of our sacrificial Lord.

At her funeral Mass, I placed it on her casket over the baptismal pall and then later took it back to my apartment to remind me that the sacraments give us *more* grace. Already, I had a Sacred Heart Badge, a medal of the Christ's Head, a sculpture of the Praying Hands, and now I possessed—the only one of its kind—*the Sacred Feet of Jesus.*

Look at my ... feet;
it is really I.

—Matthew 11:28

HONEY
The Divine Physician

Resting in the tea room, Honey sipped her coffee. Sister Amez placed a birthday cupcake on the table with one burning candle. Turning off the lights, we sang Happy Birthday to Honey.

"Where's my big cupcake cake?" Honey asked.

"That's later after dinner," Sister explained. "Now make your wish, dear."

Inhaling and exhaling, Honey blew out the one candle.

Cutting the cupcake in quarters and giving her the first piece, I asked, "Well, Honey, how's it going?"

"Fair and partly cloudy," she said.

After the weather report, even though I knew it was her 91st birthday, I inquired, "By the way, how old are you?"

She raised her index finger, saying, "I'm 'one' today."

"*One*? Are you sure?"

She nodded and grinned. "You know how it is, Father."

"No, tell me."

"You tell him, Sister."

"No, Honey, you tell him."

"Well, Father Chris, they wake you up in the morning. Take you to the bathroom. Dress you, feed you, and undress you in the evening. Then they take you back to the bathroom at night, and put you back to bed again. That's why I'm one today," she said with her childish smile.

"You're not at that stage yet," I said.

"O yeah? Last week I was—during my 'flu' bout, and I hope I never go through that again; I don't want to be treated like a baby anymore." she said. "Now how about a birthday blessing?"

Cupping her face in my hands, I kissed her forehead, blessed her and said, "Happy First Birthday!"

One day on a room visit, I asked, "How's Honey?"

Taking her hands, she slapped her face and rolled her eyes, saying, "Well, Father, some days you got 'the bear' and some days 'the bear' got you. Today, 'the bear' got me. But you don't wanna hear about my problems. You got enough of your own." Then she told me about all her ailments.

"Besides my headaches and backaches, my hair is falling out. My feet hurt, my knees quake, and my body shakes. Just this morning, Father, I met my doctor after a long wait in his busy office. Like you, he asked, 'How's Honey?'

'Hurting,' I said.'

'Where?' he asked.

'It hurts when I touch here, here, here and here,' I said, pointing to my head, back, legs and feet.

'I know what's wrong,' he said.

'What is it doc, tell me!'

'It's your finger.'

'My *what*?'

'Your finger. It's broken. I'll need to operate,' he said, laughing at me."

"Father Chris, my doctor is such a kidder."

"And you're not?"

"Me, a kidder?" she asked, looking down at my feet. "I bet I know where you got your shoes."

She couldn't know, I thought. "OK, I'll bet you a decade of the rosary; you pick the mystery."

"Let's make it a whole rosary, and you pick the mysteries," she said.

"OK, and it's to be prayed in the chapel for our special intentions. Is it a bet, Honey?" I asked still hoping to dream about heaven to dispel my fear of death.

"Fine."

"OK, tell me where I got my shoes?"

"On your feet," she said, laughing at me. "I got the doctor the same way."

"And you think he'll pay up?"

"Sure! He's good for it. He just doesn't understand my aches and pains like my primary physician who makes house calls."

"Who's that, Doctor Welby?"

"No, Father, Doctor Jesus!" she said, bowing her head. "He visits me everyday without any hassle whatsoever. And when I go to His office in chapel, there's no waiting room or forms to fill out. He'll heal me before any surgeon cuts me up. I pray He'll take me fast. Poof! Like here today, gone today."

"You're fine," I said.

"You don't understand my aches and pains either," she said. "No matter, you just pay the bet and offer the rosary in the chapel for my quick-wish intention."

"No way! I'm not giving the Lord any ideas about you. He might take you too soon from us."

"Won't that be grand. I'm ready."

"Well, I'm not ready to let you go."

"Then git ready, 'cuz when Doctor Jesus makes his last house call for me, I'll drop you like a hot potato," she said. "And make sure you pay your debt, Father."

"Hey, I'll pay, but I'll pray that God's will be done, not yours."

"Amen," she said.

Honey kept herself ready for Doctor Jesus by her sacramental life. Every day she attended Mass and received Holy Communion. Every Saturday, confession. Daily, she prayed the rosary in chapel. And every night, she kept vigil before the Blessed Sacrament praying from her devotional books that she carried around in her bag.

"What's in that bag, Honey, your money?" I asked.

"I wish. It's my bag of tricks."

"Show me."

Opening her spiritual bag, she asked, "Remember Felix, the cat?"

"You mean that cartoon?"

"Exactly." She sang: "Felix the cat, the wonderful, wonderful cat. Whenever he gits in a fix, he reaches into his bag of tricks." Grinning, she continued, "Whenever I get in a fix, I reach into my bag of tricks and pull out a divine prescription."

"Got any extras?"

She pulled out a booklet of Eucharistic prayers from the Holy Spirit Adoration Sisters, the Pink Sisters on Green Street. "Here, take this; it'll do you good," she said, shuffling her feet away from me.

"Hey, Honey, where you going?"

"To chapel, to chapel, where else?"

On another day when she was fishing through her bag of spiritual tricks, I asked, "Anymore divine prescriptions in there for me?" She pulled out a business card and gave it to me. On one side, it read:

> **JESUS, THE CHRIST**
> **DIVINE PHYSICIAN AND SON OF GOD**
>
> *Day, Night Services*
> *No Appointments Necessary*
> *Makes House Calls*

On the other side:

> *Absolutely NO Fees Required*
> *Love and Sorrows Accepted*
> *Available for Chats, Walks, Decisions, and Complaints*
> *Specializing in Ailments of the Soul, Mind, and Body*

Honey added, "And no waiting rooms or forms to fill out. He also accepts collect calls, Father, so call Him."

Within that same year, after her last night vigil, Honey called Sister Amez and complained about chest pains. After attending her, Sister left her on the rocking chair to call me. "Father, Honey's in pain," she said. "You never know; you better come."

"OK, I'm on my way."

With her death on my mind, I headed for her room. Arriving there before Sister Amez, who was getting some medication, I found Honey dead to the world with a surprised expression as if she walked into her own surprised birthday party. Poof! Just the way she wanted to go: Here today, gone today!

Looking around her room, I saw near her bag of spiritual tricks an envelope with my name on it. Opening it, I read:

THE PRIEST

A priest must be both Great and small,
Noble of spirit as if of royal blood,
Simple and natural as if from peasant stock,
A hero in the conquest of self,
A man who fought with God,
A source of sanctification,
A sinner forgiven by God, Master of his desires,
A servant for the meek and feeble,
Who does not bow before the powerful
But kneels in the presence of the poor,
Disciple of his Lord, Head of his flock,
Beggar with wide-opened hand,
Bearer of countless gifts,
A man on the battlefield,
A mother comforting the sick
With the wisdom of age and the trust of a child,
Aiming for the Most High with his feet on the ground,
Made for joy,
Familiar with suffering,
Remote from all envy, lucid, speaking candidly,
A friend of peace,
An enemy of inertia, Forever constant …
So unlike myself!

At the bottom of the page, Honey wrote, "And so much like Father Chris." My tears smudged her words.

What happened in that short period between the time when Sister Amez had left her, and when I had found her body? No one knows. But maybe, just maybe, Doctor Jesus would have surprised her by saying, "Happy First Birthday! Let's go."

"Where to, Doctor Jesus?" she might have asked.

"To heaven, Honey, to heaven, where else?" the Divine Doctor might have answered.

Receiving her final healing, Honey dropped us all like a hot potato and took her place in heaven—where else?—for her big cupcake cake to celebrate her eternal birthday with *the Divine Physician.*

People who are healthy do not need a doctor; sick people do.

—Mark 2:17

Ida

On the Right Side of Life

Inquiring point blank, Ida asked, "Father Christopher, are you registered to vote?"

"No, I don't think so. It's been over three years since I voted."

"Why so long?"

Feeling like I was going to confession, I said, "Well, Ida, I'm sick and tired of politics."

"But, it's a matter of life or death! You must support the pro-life candidates to defend the unborn children, the least of our brothers and sisters, you simply must," she insisted. "Don't be a goat, Father, vote! It's your civil duty."

"But, but I don't even know who the pro-lifers are."

"You will," she said, handing me a voter's registration form. "Just fill it out, Father Christopher, and vote on the right side of life."

"Please call me, Father Chris; I like it better."

"But Christopher sounds more priestly," she said.

"I know, but I like Chris better."

"All right, Father Chris."

Weeks before Election Day, Ida posted the names of the pro-life candidates around our home and distributed the voting literature to all the residents. For the ones who couldn't get out to vote, she passed out absentee ballots. On voting day, she went door to door, saying, "Don't be a goat; vote on the right side of life."

Casting my ballot, I walked out from behind the curtain. Meeting Ida, I said, "I feel like I just made a good confession."

"Good, Father Chris, now stay on the right side of life."

Ida did many charitable acts around our home. If she found out that someone needed something, she got it without the person knowing she did it. Often, I found toothpaste, stamps, and candy at my door. If I coughed or sneezed, my mailbox became a miniature pharmacy. My suspicion was that Ida was behind it all, and like Saint Nicholas, she eventually got caught.

"Don't you feel well, Father?" she asked me one day, after observing my misery.

"I just have a headache," I replied, but later that afternoon, I caught her red-handed stuffing a bottle of aspirin in my mailbox.

"Gotcha, Ida!"

"Shh," she said. "It's for your headache. Don't tell anyone. We mustn't let our left hand know what our right is doing."

"But what about letting our light shine?"

"It's shining now on you, Father Chris, but only by His divine exposure. Besides, I must care for His priests; I simply must."

Shortly after the Aspirin Bust, Ida was diagnosed with colon cancer and needed extensive surgery. On my next visit to her, she said, "Father, I need to share with you and ask your opinion about something." I thought she wanted to talk about her surgery. "It was a few days ago on the Feast of Pentecost," she said. "Unable to pray, I sat holding my Blessed Mother statue. Suddenly, as if watching TV, I had a dream:"

It was night!

On a hillside, I sat as a child high above Jesus, who stood at a swamp. Overhead, I saw dark shadows of sheep and goats all mixed together and fighting. Down below, near Jesus, all around the swamp, I could see all my childhood fears emerge--crocodiles, alligators, snakes, and lizards. Being paralyzed, all I could do was watch.

Suddenly, kicking off His sandals, Jesus disrobed. Wearing only a blue loincloth, He dove into the stagnant swamp. The odor was unbearable. For a while, He stayed under the slimy water. When He came up, He held a girl's body covered with swamp filth. He struggled to bring the corpse to land.

Finally on the bank, Jesus wiped away the scum from the dead girl's face and administered mouth-to-mouth resuscitation. Straining my eyes to see more, I fainted. Regaining consciousness, I found myself being the brought-back-to-life-girl in the arms of Jesus. We were covered with scum—the odor unbearable—and I was regurgitating dirty, filthy, swamp water.

Taking my hand, He led me up the hill through all the peaceful animals to a waterfall with angels holding trumpets all around. After refreshing ourselves, He spoke, "My little Ida, let's go home."

It was day!

"Father, what's it all mean?"

"I think it means that Jesus, the Light of the World, will be with you always and lead you through the darkness of life—just as He promised—especially now in your sickness and suffering. You need to trust Him."

More than I do, I thought.

"And soon, Ida, through it all the Lord Jesus will bring you home to the place He is preparing for you."

"You mean, I'm going to heaven?"

"You betcha!"

"Then, it'll be all worth it."

"For sure," I said, "and when you get there, Ida, remember my special intention."

"Certainly, Father Chris."

As the days passed, after her surgery, she suffered more and more, regurgitating several times a day. Then, on that infamous day, January 22, before dawn, Sister Amez called me to come and anoint Ida. As I entered the room, I saw Mother Vincent on the "Watch" sitting at Ida's right. Sister Amez stood at the foot of the bed, and I took my place on the left side of Ida. After celebrating the Sacrament of the Sick, we prayed the rosary, and we watched.

It was night!

Turning on her left side, Ida regurgitated green slime—the *odor unbearable!* I needed to step out. The Sisters and the aides changed her sheets and clothes. Sister Amez sprayed the room with Lysol disinfectant and invited me back. Once again, I took my place next to Ida on her left side.

Suddenly, she cringed. Lying on her left side, she took a deep breath—her pain more intense. Pushing herself up, she lifted her head and fixed her eyes above me. Her countenance, horrible! It was agonizing to see. Her anguish frightened me. It seemed as if she was glaring at the face of the devil. My heart pounced. Feeling an evil presence, I was fearful and moved to her right side. Sprinkling holy water on her tormented body, I whispered, "Please, *Jesus*, save her and me from my fear."

Slowly, she turned to the right toward me. As she did so, her expression began transforming right before our eyes. Now it seemed that she was gazing at the face of God. Her eyes fixed above us. Her angelic face radiated peace. My fear subsided.

Sister Amez opened the drapes whispering, "She's taking her place in heaven."

It was day!

Then glowing with a smile, Ida took two more breaths and died *on the right side of life*.

> **When the Son of Man comes in all His glory,**
> **escorted by all the angels of heaven....**
> **The king will say to those on his right:**
> **'Come. You have my Father's blessing.'**
>
> —Matthew 25:31,34

JENNY

And the Word Was Made Flesh

Sister Jenny caught me in my jogging clothes at the stairwell. "Is that you, Father?" she asked.

"Yes, Sister. Is it you?"

"It is."

"Then it's the two us," I said.

"Are you feeling all right?"

It just so happened that I didn't feel well that day. Expecting a little sympathy, I said, "Pray for me, Sister, I'm sick, and I'm afraid I'm not long for this world."

Lifting her stooped head higher and looking into my eyes, she said, "You're the biggest baby in the house!"

"I am?"

"Yes, you are, poor baby. Where're your priest clothes? Didn't your mother teach you how to dress? Didn't she bring you up right?"

"Yeah, she did, but I'm going for a brisk walk to feel better, I hope."

"Young man, march yourself right to your room and put your priest clothes back on. Then go walking."

"OK, Sister," I said, pretending to do so.

Year by year, Sister Jenny mellowed more and more. She became childlike. We were all attracted to her divine radiance. The peace of Christ oozed from her.

"How did you get so holy?" I asked her one day. "What's your secret?"

"Well, Father, it's the mystery of the Mass," she said. "We become what we adore the most. I adore Jesus the most in the Blessed Sacrament. A team of wild horses can't keep me away from the Holy Sacrifice. I know the victory of the Victorious Victim."

"And what's that victory?"

"We are, Father. He saves us from sin, wins us from Satan's death policy, and makes us holy like Himself so we can live forever." Leaving me, she said, "I'm offering my Mass for your special intention. God bless you, Father."

"Thank you," I said, hoping that Jesus would hear her prayer and let me dream about Him to dispel my fear of death.

Sister Jenny never permitted anything to come between her and the Mass. Once she sat outside the viewing room on the second floor waiting for Sister Amez to escort her to Mass. She said to Abby, the funeral directress, "That nun forgot me again. If she doesn't come soon, I'm going down the elevator with the corpse." And that's exactly what she did that day, rather than be late for Mass.

On another beautiful day, Sister Jenny and Sister Amez walked around the outside of the chapel. I met them in front of the wall behind the tabernacle.

"There He is!" I said, pointing beyond the holy bricks.

"Tell Father Chris where you're going," Sister Amez said.

Leaning on her cane and straightening her stooped body, Sister Jenny said, "I'm going to Mass, the wonderful, wonderful Mass."

"O Sister," I said, "I thought you were going to *heaven*?"

"Same thing," she said. "Do you know, Father, you're looking at a miracle?"

"Where?" I said, looking all around.

She poked her chest. "Me! I'm the miracle."

"Aren't we all?" I asked.

"Not like me. You see, in 1923, for two months I laid in a coma. I almost died when I was 12."

"Twelve? You were twelve?" She nodded. "How old are you now?"

"I don't know." She turned to Sister Amez. "How old am I?"

"You're 92."

"I'm that old?" she asked, looking puzzled.

"Yes, you are," Sister Amez said. "You can't remember your age, but you remember your coma dream."

"Of course, I do," Sister Jenny said, "It never changes, but my age does."

"Anyway, tell me about your coma dream," I said. "I never heard it before."

"We won't be late for Mass, will we?" Sister Jenny asked.

"Of course not;" Sister Amez responded, "Father's with us."

"Well, in 1923, I lay dying at Holy Spirit Hospital for two months, and..."

Gasping for breath, I saw the Blessed Mother wearing a white gown with a yellow sash around her waist, a blue veil, and a crystal rosary in her praying hands. Smiling, she said, 'Gracie, be not afraid and come with me.'

*Not knowing how, I found myself at the foot of the cross, surrounded by angels with trumpets. Jesus was crucified **in my dying body**—and not another. My flesh was lacerated* *on the cross; my un-bloody spirit stood with Mother Mary.*

Looking down, He said to her, 'Mother, behold your daughter; daughter behold your mother.' Tenderly, she wrapped her arms around my youthful spirit, saying, 'Your brother, Jesus, is changing all the badness into all His goodness.

'Soon, we will be in paradise,' Jesus said, squirming like a worm on the wood of the cross. 'Father, forgive Gracie, do not abandoned her, she doesn't know what she's doing.' My Savior gulped air in my dying body. As He licked my dry lips with my corruptible tongue, He continued His words, "Father, I thirst for Gracie!" Groaning, He pushed Himself up. 'Into your hands, Father, I commend my sister, your precious daughter.'

Closing my spiritual immortal eyes, I hugged Mother Mary who whispered, "It's almost over."

Hanging low in my tormented body, He swallowed hard and cried out victory:

"It's finished!" Bowing my mortal head, Jesus died my death.

"Wow, Sister, you just described the mystery of the Holy Sacrifice of the Mass in a personal way."

"Yes, Father," she said. "I know my personal Victorious Victim."

"Was it the dream that made you become a Little Sister of the Poor?"

"Yes, it's why I work for the dying souls."

"I see," I said. "Anyway, what put you in a coma?"

"It's a mystery. No one ever knew. Not even the doctors."

"How did you come out of it?"

"Well, from the Mass prayers, of course. My grandparents, parents, brothers, sisters, aunts, uncles, teachers, and friends attended Mass every day and prayed for me. And I woke up. It was a miracle! If you want to see miracles, pray the Mass."

Suddenly, a monarch butterfly fluttered by us. "It looks like the one we let go," Sister Amez said. Just then, the chapel bells rang out *How Great Thou Art.* Inspired by Sister Jenny's dream, Sister Amez and I sang in the melody of the chimes:

> *And when I think that God his Son not sparing,*
> *Sent him to die, I scarce can take it in,*
> *That on the cross, my burden gladly bearing,*
> *He bled and died to take away my sin—*

"Enough now!" Sister Jenny interrupted. "It's Mass time."

On a different one of our morning encounters, as she would often do, Sister Jenny asked, "What time's Holy Mass?"

"Eleven," I said. "It's always 11, unless it's Sunday, or another feast day, or a funeral, or something else special, then it's 10:30."

"What time did you say for today?"

"Eleven, I said."

"What time is it now?"

"Half-past nine," I said, speaking in her tell-time language.

"I better not be late," she said, "so I better get moving. God bless you, Father. Be a good boy now; I'll be praying for your intention." Clutching her rosary, she leaned on her cane and headed for chapel to take her front row seat to make her daily holy hour before Mass. Whenever she saw me leaving the building, she would ask, "Going out for Mass?" When I would answer yes, she'd beam.

Coming back from the outside, she would ask, "Coming back from Mass?" I would smile, and she would ask, "How many today?"

I was always happy when I could tell her two or three. The more I said, the more she beamed.

On one occasion, I said, "Boy, the devil is sure busy out there." I flecked my muscles. "I wish I could get the evil one by the neck and wring it like a chicken! I can't stand his guts."

As I twisted my fists around one another, she smiled and said, "That's what you do every time you offer the Holy Sacrifice of the Mass."

"I do?"

"Of course! At the elevation, the Word of God becomes flesh and you wring the devil's neck. Jesus absorbs all the evil and pours out all the good. In an instant you undo the devil's works," she said. "Your might can't hurt the devil; he'll chew you up and spit you out. But **His** power defeats Satan when you offer the Holy Sacrifice. And he hates your guts for it!"

"He does?"

"And how!" she said. "He's got your picture on his dart board."

"Stop scaring me," I said.

"Don't be afraid, you big baby, you got the power of God on your side. Use it wisely," she insisted.

Her attendance at Mass inspired us all. It was hard for her to sit up straight, but during the consecration, she held her head up high. Looking at her transfixed eyes at the elevation transcended me to Calvary. Such deep reverence and devotion to the Real Presence this world seldom sees.

On her last day, during the season of Ordinary Time, we celebrated a 4 P.M. Mass in her room. There I gathered with the

Little Sisters around the portable altar at the foot of Sister Jenny's bed. Looking at her was like seeing Christ incarnate, suffering, and dying in her body. It was all like the description of her coma dream. Only now I could see it more vividly.

During the consecration, she fell asleep. At the elevation, Mother Vincent rang the bells. She woke and fixed her eyes on our Eucharistic Lord. While we prayed the Our Father, she drifted off again. We were concerned that she wouldn't wake up for the Viaticum, her last Holy Communion. Elevating the sacred host, I said, "Behold the Lamb of God," raising my voice, I added, "the Victorious Victim who takes away the sins of the world!"

In the holy pause, I could sense all the Sisters praying for her to regain consciousness. "Saint Joseph, wake her," I silently prayed. Then those blessed bells jingled again—she woke! Sitting up, with some help, she received the Viaticum to the relief and delight of us all. "It's a Mass miracle," I whispered, "just like she said."

Immediately after the Holy Sacrifice of the Mass, she drifted into a coma. I caressed her baby face, cupped it, and kissed her sweet forehead. It was like touching the crucified face of Christ. Leaving the convent, I knew I would never see her alive again in this world. An hour later at 6 p.m. when the chiming bells struck and the Little Sisters were praying the Angelus around her, Sister Jenny dropped her head down and, just like in her dream, I knew, Jesus drew her last breaths. Peacefully, she passed over with Him to her place in heaven at these saving words: *And the Word was made flesh.*

> **The Word became flesh and made his dwelling among us,**
> **and we have seen his glory ...**
>
> —John 1:14

KITTY

Her Sacred Whisper

Tapping her cane on the floor, Kitty stood by the doors at the holy water font inside the chapel, blocking my way out.

"Sorry, Father Chris, I just stopped for a moment to peek in and say 'hello' to Jesus," she whispered, bowing her head. "Since you're here, may I have your blessing?" After blessing herself, she quoted her favorite poem:

> *Hearts, like doors,*
> *Open with ease*
> *With very, very little keys,*
> *And don't forget*
> *That two of these are:*
> *'Thank you,' and*
> *'If you please.'*

"So thank you, Father, for the blessing," she whispered, "and if you please, keep blessing me."

Reminding her of one of her favorite sayings, I whispered back, "Whenever you pass a church, make a visit; so when they carry you in, the Lord won't say, 'Who is it?'"

"Hey, that's my line!" she said.

Following her outside the chapel, I said, "Kitty, may I ask you a question?"

"Sure, Father."

"How many visits do you make a day?"

"Are you checking up on me?"

"Sure I am; it's my job." We sat on the bench. "So how many?"

"Well, not counting my 'hello visits', I make two 15-minute visits a day. But I wish I could make a holy hour once a day, like the holy residents."

"You're holy, too, you know."

"Flattery will get you everywhere, Father. But I still wish I could pray a whole hour in His Real Presence. I can't seem to last that long; I just tire out and fall asleep."

"So what," I said. "Remember how the apostles fell asleep on Jesus in his agony, and, even though their flesh was weak, how well he accepted their willing spirits?"

"Yes, I do."

"And Saint Therese, the Little Flower, often fell asleep during her communion meditation."

"She did?"

"Yes and she saw herself sleeping in the Father's arms."

"What a beautiful image," she said. "But what about Blessed Jeanne Jugan, did she fall asleep in chapel?"

"Maybe, I know she spent long hours there."

"Well, then, I guess I'll make a holy hour every day in chapel, even though if I do fall asleep."

"Yeah, that's right," I said, "just show up and stay the hour."

"I'll try."

"That's the spirit!"

A few days later we met in the tea room. "Father, guess what?"
"You made the holy hour, but fell asleep?" She nodded.
"That's OK. You were reposing in the heart of God."

"Yes, I believe that, but I made a spectacle out of myself."

"How?"

"Nodding, nose-diving, and snoring, I bothered the worshippers. Someone poked me awake. Embarrassed was I. I just can't do it. I won't distract others again from our Eucharistic Lord. I won't! The holy hour just isn't for me."

"Well, you tried."

"But, I failed."

Consoling her, I said, "Not really. You still worshipped him. Just pray as you can, not as you can't."

"Right, Father Chris. The short visits are up my alley. I'll pray as I can. I just wish I could be holy like the others."

"You may be holier."

"O my, what makes you say that?"

"Because I know your love for Jesus. You spend a lot of time in His Eucharistic presence. If you add up all your time in chapel, I bet you spend more daily time with the Blessed Sacrament than the residents who make a holy hour everyday. Let's add it up."

"Fine, you do the math."

"You say you make two 15-minutes visits a day." She nodded. "That's a half-hour. Now, I see you in church at least 15 minutes before Mass and at least 15 minutes after Mass."

"True."

"That's another half-hour or more. Daily Mass is at least a half-hour. Feast days, funerals, and Sundays, closer to an hour. And if I add up your 'hello visits', you spend more than two hours a day in His Real Presence."

"I never saw it that way."

"So maybe you're as holy, if not more so, than the others. But only God knows that," I said. "Do you know what Lillian said about you?"

"What?"

"She said she wishes she could be holy like you."

"She said that?" I nodded. "She's the holiest! She lives in the chapel."

"I know, but she fails to see her own holiness. It seems that the faithful, like yourself, are so busy seeing the holiness of others that they fail to see their own."

"Well, that's better than looking at the speck in our neighbor's eye."

"True, but it's also good to see your own holiness."

"Father, you should practice what *you* preach."

"Kitty, be grateful I don't preach what I practice."

"O my, Father Chris, now you're missing your holiness."

"Me, holy?"

With her hands funneling her mouth, she echoed my words. "It seems that the faithful, like yourself, are so busy seeing the holiness of others that they fail to see their own." I smiled. "I'm rubber; you're glue," she continued her trumpeting speech, "whatever you say bounces off me and sticks to you." Grabbing hold of her cane, she stood and tapped me on the foot with it, saying, "Let's go whisper 'hello' to Jesus for holiness."

Another day, I met Kitty coming off the elevator. Feeling inspired, I said, "Let's go say 'hello' to Jesus." Walking into the chapel, we stopped at the holy water font and blessed ourselves.

"Hello, Jesus; it's Kitty," she whispered.

"And Father Chris," I added, reverently.

When we got outside the chapel, I thought of a story that I heard and shared it with her: "Once upon a time there was a man named Jimmy. Whenever he passed a church, he stopped and just said, 'Hello, Jesus; it's Jimmy.' Then he would go his way. Right before he died in the hospital, his nurse heard a voice: 'Hello, Jimmy; it's Jesus.' She looked around and saw no one. Then Jimmy expired.'"

"I know that story," she said. "I read it in the *Catholic Digest*. It's what inspires my 'hello visits'."

"How about that! Is that odd or is that God?"

"That's God, Father."

Kitty recited her favorite saying: "Whenever you pass a church, make a visit; so when they carry you in, the Lord won't say, 'Who is it?'"

"Hey, that's my line!" I said. Smiling, I quoted her favorite poem.

> *Hearts, like doors,*
> *Open with ease*
> *With very, very little keys,*
> *And don't forget*
> *That two of these are:*
> *'Thank you,' and*
> *'If you please.'*

"So, on behalf of Jesus, thank you, Kitty, for all your visits to Him, and if you please keep making them for holiness."

"Hey, Father Chris, has anyone thanked you today for being a priest?"

"Not today."

"Well, Father, thank you!" she said, handing me a poem.

WHAT'S A PRIEST TO DO?

If a priest preaches over ten minutes, he's longwinded.
If his sermon is short, he didn't prepare it.
If the parish funds are high, he's a business man.
If he mentions money, he's money mad.
If he visits his parishioners, he's nosy.
If he doesn't, he's snobbish.
If he has fairs and bazaars, he's bleeding the people.
If he doesn't, there's no life in the parish.
If he takes time in confession to help and advise sinners,
    he takes too long.
If he doesn't, he doesn't care.
If he celebrates the liturgy in a quiet voice, he's a bore.
If he puts feeling into it, he's an actor.
If he starts Mass on time, his watch is fast.
If he starts late, he's holding up the people.
If he decorates the church, he's wasting money.
If he doesn't, he's letting it run down.
If he's young, he's not experienced.
If he's old, he ought to retire.
If he dies, there was nobody like him
And there will never be his equal again!

Throughout the years, Kitty remained faithful to her 'hello visits'. Then, on the feast of Christ the King, right after Mass, I stood outside the chapel greeting my wonderful, wonderful flock.

Suddenly, Kitty's cane flew by me, and I heard her body hit the tile floor, like a side of beef—an awful sound! Being upset and fearful of death, I knelt, took out my oils, and anointed her on the spot. I suddenly realized this was where I had told Kitty the story about Jimmy's "hello visits".

I wondered if the Savior was whispering to His holy lady, "Hello, Kitty; it's Jesus."

When the paramedics arrived, Sister Amez said, "I'm staying with her. I believe she's going home to her place in heaven."

In the ambulance, Sister Amez told us later, our holy resident regained consciousness and whispered her last two words: *"Hello, Jesus."*

> ***There was a tiny whispering sound.***
> ***When he heard this, Elijah hid his face …***

—1 Kings 19:12-13

LILLIAN

A Lily of the Blessed Sacrament

At the nurse's station sat 100-year-old Lillian in her wheelchair. Holding a cookie, she said, "Here, you, take this and eat it." Then she took her milky drink. "Take this, too, and drink it," she said. "'Tis good for you, it 'tis."

"Thanks!"

As I bit the cookie, she added, "Quick, wash it down."

I lifted the plastic cup to my lips.

"Stop!" the nurse shouted. She took the drink from me and gave it back to Lillian, saying, "Don't give your medicine to the priest."

"O, 'tis you, Fadder?"

"Aye, it 'tis," I said, imitating her brogue.

"O my, I'm sorry!" she said, making the sign of the cross. "I can't see very well, ya know."

"Now drink your medicine," the nurse said.

"What is it ye say?" she asked, bending her ear. "I don't hear so good neither."

"You heard me, Dilly Lilly. Drink it! It's good for you," she said in her ear.

"Then ye drink it. If 'tis good for me, 'tis good for you."

"It's your medicine, not mine, and you'll die if you don't drink it."

"I'll die even if I do drink it," she said in her squeaky voice. "Ye know, nurse, the Little Sisters of the Poor wouldn't treat me this way." We smiled at her.

"Now, Lillian," I pleaded, "offer it up to Jesus."

"What 'tis it you say, Fadder?"

"Give it to Jesus," I said in her ear.

"Give it to Jesus?" She bowed her head. "What kind of Roman Catholic do ye think I am? I'll never give anything like that to the Lord. Never!"

"But you gave it to me, His priest."

"I didn't know 'twas you; forgive me, Fadder, for I have sinned."

I made the sign of the cross over her, saying, "Now for your penance, drink your medicine."

"What 'tis it ye say?"

I took the medicine from the nurse and gave it to Lillian. "*Drink your penance*," I shouted. She finally gulped it down.

"Yuck! I never had a penance like that one before." Walking away, I overheard her tell the nurse. "He's a strict one, he is, but I thank God for him, because he gives us real food and drink for our souls—unlike your medicine—so we'll never die."

Lillian was known for her holiness. Even into her eighties, she still took buses and cabs to visit the shrines. She spent days and nights in churches, fasting before the Blessed Sacrament. In the chapel at Holy Family Home, it would be a rare occasion for anyone, except herself, to be alone with the Eucharistic Lord because she was there most of the time. She parked her wheelchair at the foot of the altar, gazed at the golden tabernacle, and prayed her sapphire rosary for hours and hours.

Every Saturday after Mass, Lillian came to confession. One day, she said, "O God of second chances and new beginnings, here I am again."

"How are you?"

"Miserable! I don't know why the good God puts up with me."

"Because, He loves you."

"He must to put up with the likes of me."

"Well, Lillian, look at the likes of me, and He made me a priest anyway."

"O Fadder, He loves His priests."

"He must to put up with the likes of me."

After the absolution, Lillian blessed me. She held her rosary in her shaky left hand and her steady right hand was on my bowed head, saying, "O priest of the Blessed Sacrament, ye are truly blessed. In heaven our dear Lord will put His unfading crown of glory on yer royal head. Like the tabernacle, it will glitter before the heavenly court in the holy envy of all His radiant angels. O priest of the Blessed Sacrament!" Then taking my hands, she kissed them. Looking deeply into my eyes, she continued, "Thank ye, Jesus, for absolving me; especially for giving me yourself in the Blessed Sacrament, real medicine, so I'll never die."

One day in her room, she said, "Fadder, always remember this." With her thumb and index finger, she drew a line across her neck.

"Remember what?" I asked.

"Your collar. Remember what it means."

"What?"

"It means you're a priest forever. And never forget that without the priest there's *no* Blessed Sacrament. They go together like the two hearts of Jesus and Mary."

"I know," I said.

Poking her temples with her index fingers, she said, "Know Mary, know Jesus." Continuing her wisdom, she shook her head from side-to-side and added, "No Mary, no Jesus; no Jesus, no priest; no priest, no Blessed Sacrament."

On Lillian's birthday, we offered Mass for her intentions. After the entrance hymn, I took the hand-microphone down to her, saying, "Happy Birthday!"

"What is it?" she asked, bending her ear.

"It's your birthday!" I exclaimed. "How do you feel being 101?"

"I don't feel!" she shouted. "My age sounds like a bad temperature. Now, Fadder, git on with it."

"With what?"

"The Mass, what else?"

"OK." For our communion meditation, we sang her favorite hymn:

> *Come to the banquet I have made.*
> *Take the bread and the wine I will give you.*
> *Body and blood I will give you.*
> *My life for the world I will give.*
> *Alleluia! Alleluia!*

At the age of 102, Lillian became seriously ill. For months she lingered in her sickness. We prayed for the Lord to take her home. We couldn't understand the divine delay. During the last week of her life, she could no longer eat and had to receive nourishment intravenously to prevent dehydration and to ease her pain. On the Fourth Sunday of Easter, after I anointed her, I realized that this holy woman literally lived with the Blessed Sacrament. It was said of her that she was an all-year-round Easter lily before the tabernacle.

Turning to Sister Amez, I said, "Let's wheel her into the chapel so she can be with the Blessed Sacrament."

"No, Father," she said. "It's too hard with the IVs. Besides, she's not conscious."

Well, then, I thought, if Lillian can't be with the Blessed Sacrament in the chapel, then I'll just bring the Blessed Sacrament to be with Lillian in her room. Why didn't I think of this before, I wondered. Bad effects of original sin, I figured. But grace prevailed.

In the sacristy, I got the pyx. Genuflecting before the glittering-golden-doors, I brought the Blessed Sacrament to her room in that sacred vessel that I like referring to as my little movable tabernacle. The nurse was replacing the IV bag. At Lillian's bedside, I genuflected. Leaning over her body, I placed the pyx containing the Blessed Sacrament on her chest. Suddenly, at that precise instant, Gabriel's trumpet sounded for her. Even before I could bless myself, she took a yawning breath and slowly exhaled, never to breathe again. I smelled a sweet garden around her body, and I saw a golden aura around her face.

For some reason, I thought about my first day at Holy Family Home and that attractive Bible with the ascended Lord and the angelic trumpeters on its cover. It made me confident that this beloved soul took her prepared place with Him in heaven. Still, like a frantic, blustering bee, Sister Death stung me again. However, Lillian parted from us, just as she lived, as *a lily of the Blessed Sacrament.*

If anyone eats this bread he shall live forever.

—John 6:51

MINNIE

Heaven's Apple Tree

estled in her bed, Minnie sneezed.

"God bless you," I said.

"Not good enough," she hollered. "Give me the real thing, will ya?"

"My blessing, you mean?"

"That's it," she said, folding her hands in prayer and closing her eyes.

"May almighty God bless you, the Father, and the Son, and the Holy Spirit."

Instead of the "Amen" response, she bowed and said, "Jesus, I love you."

On another occasion, Minnie sat up under the blanket holding her Bible. "Minnie, would you like my good night blessing?"

"No, I want more," she demanded.

"Well, how about the Sacrament of the Sick?"

"Yeah, that's it." After the anointing, she bowed her head and said, "Jesus, I love you."

"Minnie, Jesus loves you too, you know?"

She nodded. "Of course, I know." She held her holy book

high. "The Bible tells me so. And He loves you too, but you don't say it right."

"Well, how should I say it?"

"Say, 'Yes, Jesus loves me.'" she said, bowing her head. "Now do it."

Bowing, I said, "Yes, Jesus loves—ouch—me !" She bopped me on the head with her Bible.

"Now ya got it," she said. "And don't forgit it."

"I won't. It's pounded into me," I said.

"Good."

"Well, I better go."

"Where ya goin'?"

"To heaven," I said, "to heaven, where else?"

"Take me with ya!" she shouted.

"Do you really wanna go?"

She became all excited. "Yeah, how?"

"Go straight," I said, "and turn right."

"OK, let's go," she said, throwing off her blanket.

"Whoa! Hold your horses. We can't go now."

"When?" she asked, falling back on the bed.

"When Jesus comes." I bowed my head with my eyes on her Bible. "Only He can take us. It'll be beautiful. We'll sing, dance, and feast on the finest foods." Knowing she craved apples like I did, I added, "And we'll eat all the apples we want."

"I wanna go now!" she shouted.

"We can't. We gotta wait for Jesus to take us."

"When's He coming?"

"Soon," I said. "He's picking the apples."

"Good."

"Now, go to sleep," I insisted.

"I can't."

"Why?"

"I'm hungry!"

"Then close your eyes, turn on your right side, and think about sitting with Jesus under the apple tree. That'll help you sleep. And when ya git to heaven's apple tree, tell Jesus I want to dream about Him, too, and make sure you save some apples for me, will ya?"

"We'll see."

"Good night, Minnie, and God bless you."

"O no you don't! Give me the real thing."

"But I just anointed you."

"I want more," she said.

"What?" I asked.

"God, ya knucklehead!"

Smiling, I laid my hands on her and prayed. "May almighty God bless you again in the name of the Father, and the Son, and the Holy Spirit."

"Jesus, I love you," she responded, bowing her head and closing her eyes.

Kissing her on the forehead, I bowed and whispered, "Jesus, I love you, too." How I enjoyed this simple soul! She owned few belongings. A crucifix hung above her bed. On her bureau sat statues of Jesus, Mary, Joseph, Blessed Jeanne Jugan, Saint Jude, a few little angels and her Bible—no more.

Passing by Minnie's room one day, I heard her shout, "Where ya goin'?"

At her bedside, I answered, "Heaven, where else?"

Her eyes glittered. I thought she was going to tell me to take her along. Instead, she said, "I just came from there. It's beautiful!"

"Did ya see Jesus?" I asked, bowing my head.

"Sure did."

"You had a dream, Minnie?"

"Yep."

"I love hearing about dreams; tell me yours."

"Well, all right then:"

After I prayed, "Jesus I love you" I blessed myself, in the name of the Father, and of the Son, and of the Holy Spirit. Then, I saw Him with His mother under a tree picking apples and putting them in the fold of His garment. It was all out of this world. Every time he picked one—presto! Another one appeared. With the shiny red apples, He took my hand and led me away from His mother down the mountain to the seashore. I was a little girl. All day we walked and talked with the angels and ate the juicy apples on the beach.

"Did ya tell Him I wanted to dream about Him too?" I asked, craving an apple.

"Uh, huh," she said, bobbing her head.

"Well, what did He say?"

"Nothing, but He smiled, sang, and danced with me on the sand in the sight of the angels."

"What did He look like?"

"He looked like ..." Her pause left me in suspense.

"*Tell me!*"

"He looked just like ..."

"*What?*"

"You!"

"*Me?*"

Licking her lips, she said, "Yep, like you at Mass, and His

angels ate up all the apples that I was saving for you."

"Tell me more," I said.

"Nope, the rest is private," she insisted.

"Please, I'll give you an apple tomorrow?"

"Nope, got my own. After my dream, the Little Sisters gave me a basketful of apples for my birthday. If ya stop pestering me, I'll let ya take one," she said, pointing to her apple basket, hidden under a towel in the corner of the room.

Lifting up the towel, I grabbed an apple and bit into it. "Mmm! OK," I said. "I never refuse an apple."

As the months passed, Minnie spoke less. In her bed-chair at daily Mass, she seemed unaware, but whenever the Holy Name was invoked, she bowed her head. At communion time, instead of saying 'amen', she would always fixate on me and the host, as being one, for a long precious moment, and then sweetly say, "Jesus, I love you." I always received the blessing from her of knowing, at that sacred moment, that it was no longer I, but Jesus in His Eucharistic priesthood.

On Christmas Eve after our vigil Mass, the Little Sisters and I met in Minnie's room to pray the ritual for the dying. The little altar was set up with little angels and a Nativity scene between the two burning candles. On her night table sat a small tree blinking the red, white, and blue lights of Christmas. With the Brown Scapular and Miraculous Medal around her neck, she held a rosary in one hand and a little angel, from off the altar, in the other hand. Her Bible was tucked between her right arm and side. For our opening hymn we sang *Silent Night.* In the middle of Psalm 23 at the words, *You spread the table before me,* Minnie's color changed, and we thought she was leaving us. Immediately, I anointed her. After completing the ritual for the dying, we prayed the rosary. As we prayed the third joyful mystery, the Birth of our Lord,

I watched Minnie nodding her head ten times, fixating on me. By the fifth mystery, she became unconscious. After finishing the rosary, we sang *O Holy Night*. All the Little Sisters then retired to their rooms, except Mother Vincent who was on this "Watch".

Looking at me she said, "Father, go to bed. I'll be here."

"Thanks, Mother, but you never know. She may be going soon to her place in heaven, and I want to be here when her Divine Lover comes."

"Father, did you hear the one about her and Freddy's make-believe wedding?"

"No, tell me," I said, sitting down with her.

"Well, Debbie, the Activity Director at the time, planned the whole affair to take place under the gazebo. Your predecessor, Father Kerry was to be the marrying priest. The choir was well practiced, and the invitations, with the delicious menu, were sent out. At the rehearsal, the day before the play-around wedding, right before practicing the exchange of vowels, Minnie tore away in a huff. Catching up to her, Debbie asked, 'What's a matter?'

'Freddy tried to hold my hand,' she said.

'So, it's make-believe,' Debbie said.

'Still, Jesus might get jealous, and He's my only true love.' She took her rosary and kissed the little silver crucifix, saying, 'Jesus, I love you.'"

Chuckling over the story, I leaned over our preciousness and traced the sign of the cross on her forehead, whispering, "And, Minnie, Jesus loves you, too, you know." Sitting back on the chair, with my ruby rosary in my hands, I fell asleep.

At dawn, something or someone woke me. Minnie smacked her lips, opened her mouth, and breathed her last breaths. Bowing her head, she died gripping the rosary and her little angel. On Christmas morning, our beloved Minnie was borne into eternal life. Her face radiated delight in the golden aura of divine love. "Merry Christmas, Minnie!" Mother said.

"And Happy Easter!" I exclaimed. "Let's go on for God, Mother."

"And you to bed, Father."

With one hand on her Bible and the other on her head, I whispered, "Minnie, tell Jesus I love Him, too, and that I want to dream about Him with His angels, like you." Kissing her forehead, I added, "And ask Him, will ya, to take my fear of death away by the fruit of *heaven's apple tree.*"

He shielded them and cared for them,
guarding them as the apple of his eye.

—Deuteronomy 32:10

ℕANNY
The True Tag Man

isturbed, Nanny sat in her wheelchair and stuck out her hand. As I leaned over to greet her, she snatched my Roman collar right out of my shirt. Shaking it, she asked, "What's this?"

"You tell me," I said.

"It's a tag," she answered.

"Give it back."

"No, it's mine!" she said, whacking me with it.

"Father, let her have it for a while," Sister Amez said. "She'll put it down soon. She rarely speaks, and she's never this active."

"OK, Nanny, keep it. It's yours, but remember it's holy."

"No! I don't want it. Here, take it. "Now git!"

Fixing my collar back in my shirt, I responded, "Gladly. And thanks for giving it back."

"You're welcome, the man with the tag. Come agin."

The next day, I did stop to visit again.

"Good morning, Nanny."

She didn't respond. I took out my collar and waved it before her eyes.

"Look," I said, "my holy collar. It's Father Chris, the man with the tag, remember?" Still, she didn't react. Since it was a nice day, I took her outside for a ride in her wheelchair. Stopping at a bench, I sat down and admired creation: Breathing in deeply, I asked, "Nanny, do you smell the flowers?" She didn't answer. "Hear the singing birds? See the butterflies, the squirrels?" She ignored me. "Well, time for Mass," I said, pushing her to the chapel's balcony.

As I was leaving her, she looked up at me, and said, "You're a holy saint!"

Feeling flattered, I asked, "You mean me?"

"No, I mean, the man with the tag."

Kissing her good-bye, I said, "God bless you and please pray for my special intention." She said nothing.

Walking away, I heard her ask, "Where's the tag man going?"

On the Feast of the Baptism of the Lord, instead of the penitential rite of the Mass, I blessed the water and generously sprinkled God's people. By the time, I got to the balcony, the hymn ended. Wearing a wireless microphone and white Mass vestments, I sprinkled the sleeping Nanny. She opened her startled eyes, glared at me, slapped my holy water bucket, and shouted into my microphone, "Whatcha think ya doin'?"

"I'm sorry! I didn't mean—"

She grabbed the bucket. We wrestled. I was stronger…

"Git outta 'ere!" she hollered. "And don't come agin!"

But I had to go back and give her Holy Communion. After receiving communion myself, I prayed, "Jesus, save us both from Nanny." I feared she would slap the Blessed Sacrament out of my hand. "O God," I said under my breath, "I hope she's sleeping." Back on the balcony, however, I could see that she was wide-awake. O boy! I thought. Coming to her, I held the Blessed Sacrament in front of her eyes. She nodded.

"Body of Christ," I said, keeping a holy distance.

"Thank you," she responded smiling. While chewing the consecrated host, her blue eyes twinkled. "Come agin, Tag Man."

On a First Friday in June, I distributed Holy Communion in the balcony. Approaching Nanny I said, "Body of Christ." She beamed, but didn't open her mouth. "Nanny, Body of Christ."

She began humming and gazed upon the Blessed Sacrament. Tears flowed down her cheeks. "Open your mouth." As I held the Eucharist close to her lips, she gripped my hand and kissed the Bread of Life, three times. "It's Jesus, the Sacred Heart. Stick out your tongue," I said, sticking out mine.

"I know," she said, "but you don't. Be quiet." I gave up.

After pulling my hand from hers, I finished the communion line and was drawn back to Nanny, saying, "Body of Christ."

Sticking out her tongue, she received the Holy Eucharist and responded, "Thank you, Tag Man, come agin." I really believed that Nanny saw beyond the Blessed Sacrament and gazed upon the Risen Lord. In her childlike mind she knew she couldn't swallow Him until she saw the Sacred Host again.

Toward the end of her days, Nanny became lifeless. She barely took any nourishment. Seeing her exhausted, I carefully approached her. Although her eyes were shut, she became talkative.

"Nanny, aren't you feeling well?" I asked.

"No."

"Don't you know me?"

"No."

"It's Father Tag Man." She didn't respond. "Hey Nanny," I said, caressing her hair with my fingers. She cringed. "I'm your priest."

"I could care less."

"Do you want my blessing?"

"No, go away!"

Placing an apple in her hand, I said, "An apple a day keeps the doctor away."

Dropping the apple, she moaned, "Give me an onion a day to keep everybody away."

After giving her a silent blessing, I said, "Maybe this'll help?" Leaning over, I cupped her face in my hands and kissed her forehead. She smiled and said, "Come agin, Tag Man."

A few days later, Sister Amez called, saying, "Father, Nanny's sick. Please come. You never know."

With the Blessed Sacrament, I entered her room. She was sleeping. "Nanny, Body of Christ," I said, tapping her gently. Disoriented, she opened her eyes and focused on the sacrament. Guiding my hand to her lips, she kissed the sacred host.

"Body of Christ," I said again.

She stuck out her tongue and received Holy Communion. After kissing my hand, she chewed the sacred host, pulled me close to her lips, and said, "Thanks for coming!" Then she wrapped her hands around my neck and whispered, "Got any more apples, Tag Man?" As I stood up straight, I smiled at her. Looking confused, she asked, "Who are you?"

"I'm the Tag Man," I said, "remember?"

"No, you're not!"

Swallowing, she closed her eyes and fell asleep. Silently, I anointed her. She never stirred. On the way back to my room, I met Sister Amez.

"Father, did you forget something?"

"No, what?"

"Your collar."

Feeling around my neck, I said, "O my, in my rush, I must have forgotten it. Anyway, I'm sure Nanny didn't notice."

Early the next morning, Sister Amez woke me by phone, saying, "Father, Nanny just passed away. Please, come and bless her body."

"OK, I'm on my way," I said, looking for my missing collar. Still, I couldn't find it.

When I arrived back in her room, Sister Amez described Nanny's death:

"During the 'Watch' I noticed a shadow pass by the doorway. I got up to see who it might be. I looked up and down the hallway but saw no one. Then I heard Nanny's voice. 'You're a beautiful woman!' she said clearly. Surprised that she spoke so well, I turned around to thank her for the compliment, but I saw that she wasn't speaking to me. She sat up talking to someone at the other end of the bed.

'Who are you talking to?' I asked.

'The beautiful lady,' she said, 'and she wants to talk with you.'

'What about?'

'I don't know. Ask her,' she said, pointing at the end of the bed. Suddenly, I saw a flash of light. It was like someone taking our picture with an old fashion camera. Right then, Nanny radiated a smile, fell back on her pillow, and died. As I prayed the *Hail Mary* over her, I felt His presence and heard the sweet voice of a woman call me by my baptismal name:

'Mary Ellen?'

'Yes?'

When I got no answer, I blamed my fear, and then I called you."

"Wow!" I exclaimed. "Sister, that's a story to tell."

"Father, I wonder if I'm not long for this world."

"Hey, that's my line."

"I know, but you'll probably out live us all."

"Only God knows, Sister, the day and hour, and it could be sooner than we think, so let's be ready anyway." Even though, I feared death also, I said to her, "Be not afraid … Let's go on for God."

Taking the holy water off the little altar, I sprinkled Nanny's remains, blessed her body, kissed her forehead, and whispered, "Dearest Nanny, please pray for my special intention."

Knowing about the beautiful lady at the hour of death and that many residents die holding their rosary, I rolled down the blue blanket to see if she held anything holy. I could hardly believe my eyes—Nanny's dead hands were clutching my missing Roman collar. She died unafraid in the presence of Sister Amez, the unseen lady, and the unseen priest, the *True Tag Man*.

> **Within a short time you will lose sight of me,**
> **but soon after that you shall see me again.**

—John 16:16

Otto

When He Comes

During our talent show, I first saw Otto. The residents loved to dress up and show off. At the play many elders sang. Some told tall tales; others performed skits. Our newest resident, looking like a farmer, took center stage. In his southern accent, he recited a poem about the Second Coming of Jesus.

HE'S COMING!

There's a king and a captain high,
And he's coming by and by,
And he'll find me hoeing cotton when he comes.
You can hear his legions charging
In the regions of the sky
And he'll find me hoeing cotton when he comes.
There's a man they thrust aside,
Who was tortured till he died,
And he'll find me hoeing cotton when he comes.
He was hated and rejected,
He was scorned and crucified,
And he'll find me hoeing cotton when he comes.
When he comes! When he comes!

He'll be crowned by saints and angels
When he comes.
They'll be shouting out Hosanna!
To the man that men denied,
And I'll kneel among my cotton
When he comes.

After the applause, Otto said, "Thank ya! My grandpappy taught me it in the cotton fields back home. I was knee high." Taking his bow, he added, "God bless grandpappy!"

In the corner of his room, Otto had his worktable. There he sat, the first time I spoke to him, mending an old prayer book.

"Otto, can you give me a copy of your poem?"

"Ya liked it, Rev Father, did ya?" he asked, sitting back and rubbing his fingers through his gray hair.

"Yeah, it captured my spirit."

"Here ya go. Keep it, I got more," he said, pulling one from an old brown folder.

"Thanks! By the way, do you fix rosaries?"

"Sure do, Rev." I gave him my ruby beads, the ones Sister Christine gave me that resembled his inviting eyes. He took a tool, pinched the broken chain together, and tightened up all the loose ones. "Here ya go," he said, "like new."

"Wonderful! What do I owe you?"

"A decade of yer rosary."

"Wow! You come mighty high."

"'Cuz I do good work."

"I can see that," I said, looking over my rosary, thinking about Sister Christine. "I'll pray the whole rosary for your intentions. Keep the spiritual change."

"Thank ya, Rev. Yer mighty generous."

"You're welcome," I said. "I heard you're a convert."

"And proud of it."

"It must have been hard. The change over, I mean."

"Nope, it weren't. My wife was born Catholic and she died a good one. After we married, we wanted to be both Catholic or both Baptist for the children's sake."

"So why Catholic?"

"My wife told me I could git a bigger Bible plus sacraments and holy things, like the rosary and the priesthood; but she would lose those blessings if she became a Baptist. Ya see, Rev, I lost nothin', but gained more. I wasn't blest with children, but I was blest with the Blessed Mother and the Blessed Sacrament. Mary is the First Lady and Mother of the Eucharist, and it's the Real Presence that keeps me a good Catholic."

"Why so?" I asked, curious about his answer.

"I had a dream!" he proclaimed.

"You sound like Martin Luther King."

"Ya don't need be him to dream 'bout God."

"Otto, you gotta tell me your dream," I pleaded.

"Come, Holy Spirit," he said. "It was when I got my Confirmation and First Holy Communion at the Easter Vigil. That holy night, I got my dream:"

I was jest a boy in my dream and my heart leapt fer joy when I met Jesus on a mountaintop. He wore a white vestment. The breeze fluttered His brown hair.

'Walk with me.' He said. Close to each other, we walked to the edge. There we was a gazin' up yonder at the twinklin' stars. I felt God winkin' at me. Down at the sea, I saw moonbeams dancin' on the ripplin' waters.

'Follow Me.' He said, climbin' down the steep mountain.

'But,' I said, 'I'm only little.'

'Be not afraid. Trust Me. Come.' He said, lookin' up at me.

After climbin' down, we stood on the beach near a boat. I was dog-tired. As Jesus got into the boat, I watched. He put up the sail and sat down at the rudder. I got in and he said, 'Sit 'ere next to Me.' The wind blew up the sail and a big wave hit the boat, takin' us out to sea. Later when it got calm, He threw the anchor overboard, sayin', 'My little one, rest with Me.' In the light of the silvery moon, side-by-side, with Him gazin' into my eyes, He said, 'I love ya!'

'I love ya, too,' I said.

He took bread, cupped it in His hands, and then broke it, sayin', 'This is My body to strengthen ya for yer journey home. Take it and keep receivin' Me 'til I come agin with all my saints and angels in glory for ya.'

Gazin' in His lovin' eyes, I said, 'And you'll be findin' me hoein' cotton when Ya come.' Takin' the Bread of Life from His beautiful hands, I ate, and my dream was gone.

As I pondered Otto's dream, he remarked to me, "Rev Father, I reckon all Catholics don't know the treasure we all got inside that gold box."

"The tabernacle?"

"Yep, that's it."

"I wonder, Otto, how well I know." Envious of him, I said, "I wish I had a dream!"

"Wishin' won't do it, Rev, but prayin' might. So git yerself all prayed up and ya jest might dream about the glory of God." Pointing to the portrait of Blessed Jeanne Jugan, hanging on the wall next to his bed, he said, "Ask her to help ya have a dream 'bout the Great Sacrament, she was always gazin' at that gold box."

One hot morning, Otto tended the flowers around the garden statue of the Sacred Heart of Jesus. Seeing his sweat, I brought him a bottle of water, saying, "Break time!" We sat down on the bench.

"Praise the Lord," he said. "That's what it feels like to sit down." He slugged the water. "And I promise ya that whoever gives a cup of cold water to one of these lowly ones 'cuz he's a disciple will not want for his reward: Matthew 10:42," he said.

"You sure know the scriptures."

"Yeah, but even the devil knows the Bible from cover to cover, but for it to count fer somethin' ya gotta repent yer sins and live His word."

"Amen," I said.

"Did ya hear the one 'bout the Bible lady always callin' out its verses?" he asked.

"No."

"Well, she hollered out verses, like John 3:16. If ya didn't know it, ya hadda look it up."

"I know that one: For God so loved the world—"

"That's good, Rev Father."

"John 14:3," I said, to test him.

"And He'll find me hoein' cotton when he comes to take me to my place in heaven," he said. "Anyhow, let me tell ya 'bout that Bible lady."

"Go ahead," I said.

Wiping sweat from his brow, he continued. "One day two robbers saw the Bible lady comin' outta da bank. Them robbers ran and stole her purse. 'Acts 2:38!' she screamed. The one with the purse dropped it and ran faster than the other 'round the corner.

'Why ya drop it?' his partner asked, catchin' up to 'im.

'Didn't ya hear her scream?' he said, huffin' and puffin'. 'She hadda axe.' I laughed. 'And two 38's!'"

Laughing again, I asked, "What's that verse anyway?"

"Look it up, Rev," he said, downing the rest of his water. "I gotta git ta work and pick my cotton for the glory of God."

Later that day, I opened my Bible to Acts 2:38: "You must reform and be baptized, each one of you, in the name of Jesus Christ, that your sins may be forgiven; then you will receive the Holy Spirit."

Otto prayed and worked every day, especially in the chapel. He seemed always to be there hoeing his spiritual cotton: straightening out the hymnals, putting up the kneelers, picking up all the tissues that were dropped off the wheelchairs, and dusting the pews, even when they didn't need it. After all the work, he knelt in front of the tabernacle for a long time praising the Lord with his hands raised up. Once, when he was deep in prayer there, I noticed that his duster-hanky fell out of his back pocket. Picking it up, I handed it to him.

Smiling, he said, "Colossians 3:17." In the confessional, I took the Bible and read the verse: "Whatever you do, whether in speech or in action, do it in the name of the Lord Jesus."

On the feast day of Saint Joseph, I saw Otto feasting in the dining room. Seeing me, with his mouth full, he wrote on a napkin and held it up high for me to read: *Luke 12:37.*

The next day, to my shock, Sister Amez called me to the chapel to bless Otto's dead body. It was slumped over the last pew. The setting sun shone through the stained glass window, casting a golden aura on his face—his hanky-duster still in his hand. As I anointed his body, my tears dropped onto his bent knees. Handing me tissues, Sister whispered, "Another graduate, Father, with flying colors."

"*Summa Cum Laude*," I added.

"Mark 13:35," she said.

Blowing my nose and pondering death, I asked, "And what's that?"

"Look it up," she said.

"O yeah," I said, "and you look up John 14:3."

"I know it well, Father. I just hope I'm ready, like our Otto, when He comes to take me with Him to my prepared place in heaven."

"I can see, Sister, that he taught you real good, didn't he?"

"Yes, just like all the other graduates who have gone before him."

As Abby, the funeral directress, and her helpers, Jimmy and Johnny, took Otto's body away, Mother Vincent whispered, "He might be coming for us soon, Father. Let's go on for God."

Before leaving the chapel, I entered the confessional. Picking up the Bible, I found Sister's Gospel verse, and read it: "You do not know when the master of the house is coming, whether at dusk, at midnight, when the cock crows, or at the early dawn." Back in my room, I read the poem Otto gave me, the one he recited to us. The last paragraph made me cry.

When he comes! When he comes!
He'll be crowned by saints and angels
When he comes.
They'll be shouting out Hosanna!
To the man that men denied,
And I'll kneel among my cotton
When he comes."
—Luke 12:37

Look it up.

POLLY

The Candy Lamb Cross

Our Little Sisters brought Polly from a shelter to join our community. Because of her facial warts and her mental challenge, many people shied away from her, even though her spirit bore the beauty of a child. Most of the time, she craved attention and candy. One day she wiggled her index finger at me, saying, "Hey, come 'ere, come 'ere, will ya!"

"What's a matter, Polly?"

Pointing the finger at the innocent janitor, she said, "That one over there, 'im. He hit me!"

"Who, Jimmy?"

"Yeah, 'immy!" she said, making a fist at the window-washer, who didn't hear her. That's the one. He called me a dirt-bag." Tiny tears flowed down her bumpy cheeks.

"That's low-down!" I clamored. "I'll talk to him."

"Good, tell 'im go ta da devil, will ya."

"Now, I can't do that, Polly. Besides, he's sorry."

"No, he ain't!"

I called over to the house cleaner: "Jimmy, come 'ere, come 'ere, will ya!" Winking at him, I asked, "Are you sorry?"

"Yeah, I didn't mean it, Polly, I'm sorry!" he said, winking at me.

"See, I told you," I said.

Polly waited for Jimmy to go back to his work. "I'll knock 'im outta the winda, the dirty low-down."

"Now, now, Polly, let me give you my blessing."

"What! I ain't no Catholic," she said. I laid my hands on her head to bless her—"Comin' ta dinner with me?" she asked, interrupting my prayer.

"You buying?" I asked. She nodded. "I'll be there."

"Ya better be," she said. "Now give me a kiss, will ya?"

"Sure," I said, kissing her on the crown of her head.

Before joining her at the dinner table, I wrote a fake bill and asked the server to give it to Polly after our meal. All during the supper, I kept saying, "I ain't paying for this. You are, right, Polly?"

"What! I ain't got no money."

"Well, somebody better pay, 'cuz I ain't goin' ta no jail."

Our server waved the bill at Polly. "Who's paying this?"

"She is," I said, pointing at Polly. The server placed the pretend $18.75 check in front of her.

"What! What!" She swallowed down her ice cream, grabbed her walker, and tore out of the dining room, like a run-away robber.

The next time I saw her, she asked, "Comin' ta dinner?"

"What! What!" I responded. "You beat the bill, and they locked me up. The cop handcuffed me and threw me in jail. I had to spend the night there. And you didn't bail me out. Mother Vincent had to come and pay my bill, 'cuz you sped away like a bank robber."

"What! What! I ain't got no money." A little tear flowed down the side of her nose. "Do ya still love me?" she asked.

"You know it!" I said, kissing her.

"Comin' ta dinner?"

"You treating?"

"What! What! I ain't got no money."

"Then who's paying?"

"Yer Mutter Vincent."

On Halloween, the Little Sisters gave big bags of candy to the residents to give out to the visiting children. That day my nieces and nephews knocked on Polly's opened door.

"Whatcha want?" she asked, stuffing the candy into her mouth with chocolate all over her face. Next to her was the candy she didn't like. You could tell them, they were the bitten ones.

"Trick or treat!" my beloved relatives chanted.

Pointing at the spit-out candy, Polly said, "Take them and git outta 'ere, will ya!" Leaving her and the wasted candy, my loved ones ran off to the next room. "Ungrateful kids!" Polly shouted. "Don't come back 'ere any more!"

The nurse's aide, hearing the commotion, rushed into the room. "Where did you get the candy, Polly?" she asked, taking it all away.

"From Father's Mutter Vincent. It's for the kids. Give it back!"

"No, you had enough."

"I'm tellin'," she said. "Ya no good! I'm callin' the cops ta handcuff ya and throw ya in jail for the night. Ya be sorry, ya low-down!"

Somehow, Polly found out about the candy stored in the last pew of the chapel. I think Sister Amez stocked the drawer with a daily ration of treats for our candy lover to come in and pray. And daily, for the candy, she came, praising God in her own way. Once while praying, I heard the chapel doors bang. On her walker, Polly made a beeline, charging for the candy. She didn't take holy water, she didn't bless herself, she didn't genuflect, and she didn't bow.

She sat right down, took the candy from the drawer, unwrapped them piece by piece, and threw the papers on the holy floor. With her twinkling green eyes on the crucifix, she jammed the candy into her mouth and sucked away. Then, like a train off its tracks, Polly busted back out through the chapel doors. After a good reverent laugh, I thought that if another resident violated our place of worship like she did, I would be furious. But it was our Polly. I excused her because she was mentally challenged, and I loved her unconditionally. Then something dawned on me. Compared to God, I thought, we all suffer from being mentally challenged, and I should love everyone, including myself, unconditionally, like I do our Polly. And maybe, just maybe, God laughs at us like I do at our 'candy lover'.

One evening, I joined Polly again for supper. Being late, I asked, "Did ya pray yer grace?"

"What! What! I ain't no Catholic."

"You sure?"

"I ain't no Catholic!"

"Then, why did you receive Holy Communion last Sunday, if you ain't no Catholic?"

"Cuz, I thought you was given out candy."

"O Polly, Jesus ain't candy."

"I'm sorry," she cried. Wiping her tears away like a little girl, she asked, "Do ya still love me?"

"Yeah, you know it!" I said, patting her back. "Are you paying for the supper?"

"What! What! I ain't got no money. Ask yer mutter," she said. "Still love me?"

Leaning over the table, I cupped her face in my hands and kissed her three times on the forehead, warts and all.

"You know it!" I said. As I started to walk away, she asked,

"Where ya gone?"

"Well, I'm not long for this world," I said. "I'm gone to heaven with you."

"What! What! I ain't no Catholic."

"But you love Jesus, don't ya?"

She nodded. "Will He give me candy there?"

"All you want," I said.

Easter Monday morning, the nurse's aide found Polly dead in her chair in the middle of two colorful—torn apart—Easter baskets. On her lap sat a half-eaten chocolate cross bearing the figure of a lamb. Her face radiated a chocolate-covered smile. Although she wasn't a Catholic, the sacrificial Lamb of God, I do believe, came suddenly to Polly, not in the form of bread, but in the form of *the candy-lamb cross.*

Father, forgive them;
they do not know what they are doing.

—Luke 23:34

QUEENIE
Party Place in Heaven

naware of me watching her, she sat in the smoking room with a cigarette and a highball. Seeing me through the doorway, she waved, saying, "Hello, I'm Queenie from Florida visiting my daughter, you know, Sister Teresa. She's a Little Sister of the Poor." she said, blowing out smoke. Come in and we'll make a party for two." Stepping inside, she added, "You must be Father Christopher."

"Yes, I am, but please call me Father Chris; I like it better."

Inhaling her smoke and sipping her whiskey, she continued, "I confess, Father Chris, I'm a party person."

Seeing a tiny wooden statue of the Sacred Heart of Jesus on the table in front of her, I picked it up, saying, "And let me guess … He's the party-maker, right?"

"That's right." She licked her lips. "Can you imagine the party in heaven?"

"No, not really."

"Father, I've dreamt about it."

"Can you share it?" I asked, sitting down.

"Certainly," she said, putting out her cigarette. "One time, after praying the rosary, I fell asleep and had a dream:"

Jesus and I were walking through a dark valley, but I wasn't afraid, for He was at my side. I was a little girl, and He held my hand. Coming into the light, we crossed over a green pasture. I could see a castle up ahead and a drawbridge lowering down before us. The Lord led me across and then brought me into a magnificent banquet hall: black marble floor, white marble walls, and a blue marble ceiling with a diamond chandelier. Around a long cedar table, I saw my deceased loved ones, angels, and saints feasting to their heart's content. The Lord Jesus Himself pulled out my chair for me to sit down, and He even served my favorite food. First came the appetizers: clams casino and French onion soup. Next, the main course: lobster tail and butter sauce, stewed tomatoes, macaroni and cheese, and a baked potato with sour cream. And, saving the best for last, dessert: strawberry short cake with plenty of whipped cream and a cherry on top.

'This is only a taste of what shall be yours someday soon,' He said. 'In the meantime, be faithful.'

Standing up, I implored Him, 'Please Lord, give me something special from Your table that will strengthen me to be faithful to You?'

He smiled and replied, 'You already have Me in my Most Blessed Sacrament, real food and drink, to strengthen your faithfulness.' As He gazed into my eyes, my dream ended.

A few months later, for health reasons and to be near her daughter, Queenie moved to Holy Family Home as a resident. Blessing her room, I noticed on her table that tiny wooden statue of the Sacred Heart of Jesus. Pointing at it, I said, "There He is!"

She picked it up, kissed it, and wrapped her fingers around it. Fisting it on her heart, she said, "He's preparing a place for me in heaven."

"I know," I said, remembering her dream.

Holding the little Jesus before my eyes, she said, "Father Mike, the Norbertine, would always say as I felt." She quoted:

> *Friends will come,*
> *friends will part,*
> *but, I'll never leave*
> *the Sacred Heart.*

One Sunday, Queenie visited her brother and attended Mass at his parish church, Saint Bernard's. The next time Queenie saw me, she told me all about that Sunday's homily:

"In his sermon, the priest asked the congregation, 'How many of you want to go to heaven?' All the hands in the church went up. Then Father asked, 'How many want to go today?' All the hands went down, except one—mine. Looking at me, sitting between my brother Vince and sister-in-law Peg, he asked, 'Are you sure, madam? It's a one-way trip, you know,' he said.

With my hand still raised, I exclaimed, 'Wonderful! 'My bags are packed and I'm ready to go.'"

Piercing me with her joyful eyes, she said, "Father Chris, that priest had me going. I mean, he really had me going."

"Well, my hand would have gone down, too, and I'm glad you didn't leave us for the party in heaven."

"But I will, Father, O, I will, and so will you."

"But I'm not ready like you," I said.

"Then, get ready, get set, and go."

One day Sister Teresa called me and said, "Mom's going to the hospital. Please come and anoint her."

"OK, I'm on my way."

Right after the anointing, Queenie said, "Thank you, Father, for being a priest." The paramedics came and lifted her onto the stretcher. Before they wheeled her out, she clamored, "Where's my little Jesus? I won't leave home without Him."

"Here He is, mom."

"And my rosary, too," she said, pressing her wooden king on her heart.

"Where is it?" her daughter asked.

"Under the pillow where I keep my spiritual treasures."

Taking the rosary, Sister wrapped it around her mother's hands, saying, "Here, never leave home without it."

"Are we ready now?" asked the impatient paramedic. Gripping her sacramentals, Queenie quoted her favorite saying of Pope John, XXIII: "My bags are packed and I'm ready to go."

"Where are they?" the paramedic asked,

"In my heart," she said, instructing the ignorant.

A few days later, Queenie was sent home from the hospital with an oxygen tank hooked up to her wheelchair, but she still looked beautiful—not one of her blonde hairs was out of place. She wore glittering earrings and golden frame glasses; aromatic perfumes filled her room, and her dress was worthy of a queen. Taking her hand, I kissed it, and said, "Queenie, you look like you're going to a royal party."

"And you know where, Father."

On the feast of Corpus Christi, Queenie was confined to her bed. During our Eucharistic procession on the third floor station, Sister Teresa pulled on my cope, whispering, "Please come and let Jesus bless mom."

Nodding, I followed Sister to her mother who was sitting up in bed grasping her rosary and her little Jesus. Seeing me holding the Blessed Sacrament, Queenie's face radiated the joy of His Real Presence. Placing her sacramentals on her lap and leaning over, she wrapped her arms around the sacred monstrance and kissed the luna that contained the Eucharistic King. It was a long precious moment. Then she sang:

> Sweet Sacrament, we thee adore!
> Oh make us love thee more and more!
> Oh make us love thee more and more.

On the memorial of the Immaculate Heart of Mary, the day after the feast of the Sacred Heart of Jesus, at 2:30 A.M., Queenie became seriously sick. She told Sister Amez to call me, Sister Teresa, and Mother Vincent. On her deathbed, she clutched the little Jesus in one hand and her beads in the other. After we prayed the prayers for the dying, Queenie drifted into a deep sleep.

Returning to my room, I clutched my rosary, praying myself to sleep with a special intention to Saint Joseph for her happy death. At 5:30 A.M.. the phone rang and woke me. Picking it up, I heard Sister's voice, "Mom's in heaven, and I know she's praying for your private intentions. (Which were to have a mystical dream and take my fear of death away.) Please come and bless her body."

"OK, I'm on my way."

Back in the room, I blessed Queenie's body with holy water and kissed her glorious grin. Looking at her religious daughter, I asked, "Do you think there are any more spiritual treasures under mom's pillow?"

Immediately, Sister checked and pulled out a holy card of the Ascension, trimmed in gold, with a poem on the back of it. She read it to me:

I HAVE A PLACE IN HEAVEN

Please don't sing sad songs for me.
Forget your grief and fears,
For I am in a perfect place,
Away from pain and tears.
I'm far away from hunger,
And hurt and want and pride,
I have a place in heaven,
With the Master at my side.
My life on earth was very good,
As earthly lives can go,
But Paradise is so much more
Than anyone can know.
My heart is filled with happiness,
And sweet rejoicing, too.
To walk with God is perfect peace,
A joy forever new.

The holy card of the Ascension made me think back to my first day at Holy Family Home when I saw that attractive Bible. I could still see it, clear as day, the ascended Lord surrounded by His angels on rose-tinted clouds receiving all His graduates. Also, those precious verses of John 14:3, about our prepared place in heaven, echoed in my heart.

Queenie's body was buried next to the remains of her beloved spouse. The marble tombstone, already erected after her husband's interment, depicted the Sacred Heart of Jesus and the Immaculate Heart of Mary. The two-heart monument proclaimed to us that Queenie took her *party place in heaven.*

I am indeed going
to prepare a place for you,
and then I shall come back
to take you with me,
that where I am you also may be.

—John 14:3

Rocky

Master of Meditation

Glancing into Rocky's attractive room one morning before Mass, I had to enter and visit him. Sacramentals crowded his living space everywhere. Atop his bureau sat the images of the Sacred Heart of Jesus, the Blessed Mother, Blessed Jeanne Jugan, Saint Joseph, and angels galore. On a little table sat an old tattered Bible, and above his kneeler hung a crucifix that had faded-red markings, depicting the Lord's bloody lacerations.

"O Father, thanks for coming. How are ya?"

"Hanging in there," I said, looking at his attracting crucifix. "But I don't think I'm long for this world."

"Ha! Compared to me, Father, you're just a boy." Picking up a bottle of holy water in one hand, he swept the room with the other, introducing me to his spiritual flock. "Please bless my holy things again, and my room, too."

"OK, but why so many?"

"For my meditations, of course."

Sprinkling all around, I blessed him, the room, and his sacramentals again. From his pocket, he pulled out three one-dollar bills. "Here, Father, take one, you're worth it."

"No, Rocky, thank you, anyway," I said. "I'd rather have

something to help me meditate."

"I got just the thing," he said, stuffing his money back into his pocket. From his closet, he took a golden Holy Spirit pin from the lapel of his suit jacket and gave it to me. "There, you can't meditate without the Third Person of the Blessed Trinity," he said. "You can't even say 'Lord' without the Holy Spirit. Now, let's go to Mass."

Rocky's daily ritual before Mass entertained us. Before the statues of the Holy Family, he would meditate: He would kiss Mary, caress baby Jesus, and pat Joseph's arm. He made the sacred images look alive. There, in our silent presence, he would stand motionless. Ending his ritual, with his eyes closed, he would often knock Joseph's staff to the floor. Sister Teresa would stand by to set it in place again.

After Night Prayer, one Tuesday, I felt the world on my shoulders and the devil on my back. In the balcony of the chapel, I saw Rocky before the life-sized statue of the Sacred Heart. Standing on his toes, he stretched up his neck, like a turtle, and placed his head under the palm of our Lord's plastered left hand. Reaching for the Lord's exposed heart, he closed his eyes and caressed it. Not knowing I was behind him, I heard him whisper, "Sacred Heart of Jesus, may I have Your blessing?"

"And bless me, too, Jesus," I whispered.

Somehow, I sensed that even though Rocky's was touching the blessed plaster, his innermost being was really touching the Most Sacred Heart of Jesus, the source of all blessings. As he turned around, he saw me. "O Father Chris, I'm glad you're here."

"So am I," I said. "Can you teach me how to meditate like you?"

"Me, Father, teach you?"

"Sure, Rocky," I said, walking away with him. "I want to pray like you, because the devil is prowling like a roaring lion looking for me to devour."

"Well, in that case," he said, "I do a four-step meditation dance with sacred images, especially the crucifix—and the bigger the better."

Off to the left was the viewing room for our deceased residents. I led him there to the wall crucifix that hung next to an image of the Sorrowful Mother. Dancing with four steps, I said, "Show me — 1, 2, 3, 4."

Looking up at the top of the crucifix, he asked, "Father, do you know what the *I N R I* stands for in English?"

"In English?" He nodded.

"No, what?"

"I'll Never Regret It!"

"That sounds like Him all right," I said. Taking the crucifix off the wall, I placed it in his hands. "Now show me how you meditate."

Before his four-step dance, he sang, *Come Holy Ghost*. After the hymn, he said, "It's simple: Step One, I behold the crucifix." Holding the crucifix closer to his face, he focused on the Lamb of God. "Step Two, I caress His wounds and kiss them." As he did this, he continued, "Step Three, I close my eyes and see the Crucified One through faith." He closed his eyes. "Step Four, with my eyes still closed, I repeat Step Two in love, caressing and kissing His wounds for real in the Calvary of my heart." Handing me the crucifix, he closed his eyes again and made caresses and kisses in the celestial air. With his hands suspended and lips puckered, he became motionless.

"Rocky!" He didn't respond. I hung the crucifix back on the wall.

"Earth to Rocky," I said. "Come in, Rocky!" Still, he didn't react. His appearance changed to terror then to peace. After a while, I poked him from his trance. "What happened?" I asked.

"You scared the heaven into me. I didn't know if I should anoint you, or call 911."

"Wow!" he said, rubbing his eyes.

"Rocky, tell me, where did you go?"

"Well, if you must know," he said. Taking a deep breath, he sat on one of the chairs and began sharing his mystical experience:

My guardian angel took me on a voyage. I was young and guilty of sin. The rushing wind swelled the sails of our boat, and we cruised to a shore. Hopping down, I followed my angel, making tracks on the sandy beach and gazing at the high sand dunes in front of me, wondering about that other side. As I turned back around, the boat was gone and so was my angel, marooning me on the island.

Sounding from that other side, I heard melodious birds. A gentle force made me walk the beach line. Smelling the salted air, I looked back to see my tracks.

Suddenly, a roaring growl made me spin around. Near me, I saw a ferocious lion trapped in a steel cage. Becoming frightened, I dashed the other way; mysteriously, I ran right into the lion. Jumping back, I saw myself before the jaws of death. The gate slammed shut, locking me inside. Only salvation mattered.

Cornered by the beast, I had no retreat. The lion kicked its back feet, ready to pounce upon me. Gaping at its slobbering jaws, I regretted all my sins. 'O God, into your hands, I commend my spirit!' I prayed. 'Save me, Lord!'

Just then, Jesus appeared. He was in my old body wearing white Mass vestments.

He opened the cage, and got behind the lion. He grabbed its tail, holding the lion back, so I could get out of the death chamber. As I inched my way by the beast, it growled, snagged my shirt, and ripped it. Barely, I escaped, but Jesus did not. Safely outside, I witnessed the killer animal turning on the Lord. It was horrible!

The wild creature clawed and clawed, wounding Him in my old feet, hands, and side that He possessed, blood staining His vestments. I watched Him gulp my last old breaths and die. Sobbing, I cried out, 'Jesus, why did you take my place? I deserve to die, not you!' Hating the lion, I searched for a weapon to kill it. By the dunes, I found a spear-like stick and sharpened it off a boulder. I intended to hurl it, through the bars, into the lion's heart.

*Like a savage, I ran back to the cage. Wiping my tears away, I could hardly believe my eyes: The Risen Lord—in my **young** glorified body—sat next to the tamed lion, stroking its mane. Inviting me inside, He said, 'Come in, Rocky, and pet the cat.' Heaving the spear into the sand, I stepped inside the cage. Behind me the gate shut, but it didn't matter, I was with the Lord of Life. Next to Jesus, I reached over and, with the tip of my index finger, brushed the lion's waggling tail, saying, 'Now, kitty cat, be nice.'*

Still being in my young body and in his glory wounds, Jesus swung open the steel gate, and the three of us strutted from the death chamber. Slamming the gate, my personal Savior shattered the cage to pieces, like a pane of glass. Then, like a kitten, the lion pranced over the dunes, and together we followed...

Full of suspense, I asked, "Well, did you go over?"

"Shucks, Father!" he exclaimed. "You poked me and woke me from my unfinished dream."

"Rocky, pray for my special intention," I said, longing for my own dream.

"You're always in my prayers, Father."

Nine months later, on the feast of the Holy Cross, Rocky was dying, with his sacramentals surrounding him. The brown and the green scapulars were pinned to his pillow, around his neck hung seven medals, and in his hands, he held a crucifix with the 'I N R I' on it. Taking his bottle of holy water from atop his Bible, I sprinkled him and began the prayers for the dying. After celebrating the Sacrament of the Sick and granting the plenary indulgence, the Little Sisters, some residents, a nurse's aide, and I prayed the rosary.

As we watched, I knelt on his kneeler below his wall crucifix, rubbed my Holy Spirit pin, the one he gave me, and squeezed my little Saint Joseph statue, the one Sister Christine gave me. Reaching up to his crucifix, I looked upon the Lamb of God and caressed the faded-red markings that symbolized our Lord's lacerations. Standing up, I kissed the sacred wounds of Christ and touched the 'I N R I'. Closing my eyes, I repeated the same ritual in spirit (step number two).

"He's graduating to his place in heaven," Sister Amez said, distracting me.

As Rocky was dying before us, I could no longer see him. All I could see was Jesus Christ crucified. He pushed himself up and down in his bed. His eyes rolled around. His head turned back and forth. Like a fish out of water, he gulped air. As I placed my hands on his, my heart knew—by his shared dream—that I was touching the dying Christ. But still, I wanted more than that spiritual experience. I longed to see the Lion of Judah, like Rocky and the other dreamers: Betty, Freddy, Ida, Minnie, Nanny, Otto, and Queenie, so I could ask the Risen Lord, myself, to devour my death and the fear of it.

In the holy silence, Rocky stopped breathing. After a long pause, he took two more breaths, and I saw Jesus, with the eyes of faith, breathing those last breaths. It was finished!

Whispering in my ear, Sister Amez said, "With flying colors."

"*Summa Cum Laude*," I responded.

At the death of Rocky, I believed that I had a personal intercessor in heaven praying for my special intention. Bowing down, I kissed the body of my *master of meditation*.

> **Happy the man who meditates upon these things,**
> **wise the man who takes them to heart.**

—Sirach 50:28

STEPHANIE

The Bank of Divine Providence

L ooking through the window of the tea room, I saw her in the garden watering the flowers. With a tray of tea cups and cookies, I walked outside to the picnic table, sat down, and announced, "Sister Stephanie, tea time!"

"Dear Father, I was just thinking about a nice cup of tea," she said, wiping her hands on her apron. Sitting down next to me, she sipped her warm drink, nipped her cookie, and then sang:

TEA PARTY SONG

I like a nice cup of tea in the morning,
for to start the day you see.
And at half-past eleven, well,
my idea of heaven is a nice cup of tea.
I like a nice cup of tea with my dinner,
and a nice cup of tea with my tea,
and when it's time for bed,
there's a lot to be said,
for a nice cup of tea.

Ending the song, she said, "Father Chris, you're a Godsend." She quoted Blessed Jeanne Jugan, saying, "Blessed be God! Thank you, my God." After finishing her tea, she added, "And thank you, too, Father. Know that I pray for your intentions."

Standing up, we walked around to the grotto. Between the beds of flowers, and in front of Our Lady of Lourdes statue, Sister spoke once again in the words of Blessed Jeanne: "Let us say a Hail Mary together; it'll bring us to heaven." After honoring Our Lady and thanking God, Sister took her clippers and cut off a blooming red rose from its bush. Speaking like her foundress, she asked, "Do you know who made this?"

"God," I said.

"Yes, indeed, and He made it just for you."

As she gave it to me, I pretended to sneeze. "Achoo!"

"God bless you and blessed be God!"

Back at the tea room, Sister Stephanie gave me a tall glass of water for my rose and offered me some fruit from her basket.

"I never refuse an apple," I said, biting into it. Sitting down, she had another cup of tea and told me a story about a mystical rose:

"Once upon a time, a gardener gave special care to a particular rose. He shaded it, watered it, and even sang to it. Each day he couldn't wait to arrive at work and see its added beauty. Then one day, hoping to see it in full bloom, he hurried to the garden and saw that someone had snipped it. Angrily, he took his complaint to the master of the estate.

'Someone cut off my rose!' he raged.

'Hush!' said the master, 'I got it. It belongs to me!'"

Sister Stephanie was a virtuous woman with a great trust in divine providence. As the beggar for the community, she always brought back an abundance of goods; always she received more than needed.

One day the new manager of the Pepsi Cola called her saying that they were going to drop Holy Family Home down to only seven cases of soda a month. In her sweet voice, Sister Stephanie responded, "O my, that'll never do. The old people get very thirsty. Please reconsider us; our soda must increase not decrease."

When I heard about the possible cut back, I was concerned that I wouldn't get any more soda for my mission house in Saint Gabriel's Parish, where I minister to needy people. Meeting Sister Stephanie, I asked, "Is it true about Pepsi cutting back our soda rations?"

"Well, Father, there's a new manager, and he doesn't know us yet. But don't worry, God always provides, especially through our patrons, Saint Joseph and our dear Jeanne. This morning, I placed empty Pepsi cans in front of their statues." As she spoke, I rubbed the little Joseph in my pocket. "We won't go thirsty, Father, especially the poor ones at your ministry. However, once in a while, we get a shake-up call, because God desires us to trust Him, like Mother Mary, Saint Joseph, and Blessed Jeanne Jugan of the Cross."

The next day the manager called back, saying, "Sister Stephanie, our company reconsidered. The Little Sisters of the Poor are now our 'Number One Charity'."

From then on, every few months, Holy Family Home received at least ten skids of soda from Pepsi Cola. It would all be shared with the poor throughout the area. After Sister told me the good news, she smiled and quoted Blessed Jeanne: "It's so beautiful to be poor, to have nothing, and to await all from God."

"He's so good!" I said, quoting Blessed Jeanne Jugan.

"Yes, we only need to trust in His divine providence."

"Sister Stephanie, thank you for being a Little Sister."

"And thank you, Father, for being a priest."

On March 31st that year, I felt apprehensive over the 'Shingles'. Because of my sickness, I didn't preach that day. Later in the afternoon, I met Sister Stephanie in the garden. Sensing my fear, she asked, "Father Chris, are you OK?" she asked, putting down her water pail.

"I don't think I'm long for this world; the 'Shingles' are getting worse," I said. "Could I die from them?"

"I don't think so, Father, but be prepared anyway." Knowing my increasing fear, she pointed to the robin perched on the statue of the Sacred Heart of Jesus, saying, "Look, Father, at the little bird sitting upon Jesus' hand. It never worries."

"Yes," I said, "and I'm far more valuable than it."

"You truly are!" She told me—in that sweet voice—another one of her stories. "Once upon a time some British workers saw a bird's nest under a railroad bridge. Quite peacefully, the hen sat on her eggs as the passenger trains sped and roared over top of her. Inspired, someone wrote these verses:

> *Said the robin to the sparrow,*
> *'I should really like to know,*
> *Why these anxious human beings*
> *Rush about and worry so!'*

> *Said the sparrow to the robin,*
> *'Friend, I think it must be,*
> *That they have no heavenly Father*
> *Such as cares for you and me.'*

"So, Father, don't worry, be happy," Sister exhorted me. "And, for goodness sake, don't miss heaven for the world. Just go and do what Jeanne Jugan tells us to do with our concerns."

"What's that?" I asked.

She quoted one of the popular sayings of her foundress:

Jesus is waiting for you in the chapel.
Go and find Him when your strength
and patience are giving out,
when you feel lonely and helpless.
Say to Him: 'You know well what's
happening my dear Jesus. I have only You.
Come to my aid...' And then, go your way.
And don't worry about knowing how you are
going to manage. It's enough to have told our
good Lord. He has an excellent memory.

The next day, the first of April, I began my homily, saying, "Yesterday, I received compliments about my homily. I heard these praises: 'Good sermon, Father! You're improving! Keep up the good work! You're getting better!' At first I felt flattered, until I realized that I didn't preach the day before." Looking serious, I continued, "Since I am a good preacher when I don't preach, I will never again give another homily here at Holy Family Home. Never!"

Walking to the altar, I bowed to it, turned around, and saw all the startled faces. *"April Fools!"* I exclaimed. Hardy laughter erupted.

Right after Mass, Sister Stephanie came rushing into the sacristy. "Father Jim from Saint Gabriel's just called," she said, huffing and puffing. "He's waiting for you to help him with the school's confessions."

Cringing, I overreacted by bellowing, "What? O no! I thought it was next Tuesday."

"*April Fools!*" Sister howled.

"Whew," I said. "Blessed be God! Thank You, my God."

"Happy feast day!" she jested. "Don't worry, be happy, Father Chris, we're all fools for Christ," she said, handing me an apple which I happily savored.

Months later, Sister Stephanie and I had a cup of tea on the patio. "Isn't the tea wonderful," she said. "Father, the doctors found cancer in me, and I have a weak heart. I'm not long for this world."

"Hey, that's my line," I said. She smiled. "I was stunned at her forthrightness. "Aren't you afraid?" I asked.

"Not at all," she said. "I have a trust fund in the Bank of Divine Providence. Just bless me, Father. I'll be all right."

After anointing her, I said, "Let's go on for God."

"You really know our foundress."

"Yes," I said. "You taught me well."

The following June—First Friday—Sister Stephanie was found dying outside in the flowers at the base of the Sacred Heart statue. By the time I arrived, she had died. After I conditionally anointed her warm body, Mother Vincent told me her last prayerful words:

"Eternal Father, open your gates today. O Mary, my dear mother, come to me. Good Saint Joseph, pray for me. Sacred Heart of Jesus, I place my trust in Thee."

For a while, I stood there motionless. The robins were chirping on the branches above. Sister's silver water pail glittered in the sun with her teacup tipped over beside her. Breathing in the fragrance of the beautiful roses, I admired the angelic aura around her serene face. As I gazed around, Mother Vincent asked, "What are looking for?"

"A butterfly," I said. "The symbol of the resurrection.

Wouldn't it be miraculous, Mother, if one fluttered by?"

"Yes, it would give me the spiritual chills, but that'll be the day."

"You mean the 'God Bumps'" I said. "Mother, my priest friend, Father Roland, once shared with me that a monarch butterfly—flapping its glorious wings—landed on his father's casket at the cemetery to the delight of all."

"But, Father, if you'll looking for it, you'll never see one; it's the divine surprise that makes our hearts burn within us," she said. "Let's go on for God; He may be coming for us soon."

"You're scaring me," I said.

"Father, be not afraid."

Back in the tea room, I wondered, how could God let Sister Stephanie die like a bee among the flowers and the trees? "Hush!" I whispered to myself. "He got her. He wanted her for Himself. She belongs to Him." Sipping my tea alone, I reasoned by faith that Sister Stephanie must be having her cup of tea with the "Divine Three" in her place in heaven, but only after cashing out her trust fund from *the Bank of Divine Providence*.

Blest is she who trusted that the Lord's words to her would be fulfilled.

—Luke 1:45

TESSIE

Crystal Rosary

t the third floor lounge, I blessed one of the maintenance workers. Tessie, with her crystal rosary wrapped around her hands, noticed what I was doing, and asked, "What about me? Don't I count?"

"Sure, you do," I said, blessing her too.

"Thank you, Father," she said. "What's the name of that disease when you forget everything?"

"Alzheimer's."

"That's the one. Do you know that the second thing to go with that sickness is your memory?"

"Well, what's the first?"

Looking puzzled, she answered, "I don't remember."

After laughing, I said, "Well, I hope you forget your sins like Jesus forgets them."

"Jesus forgets, too?"

"Only our sins."

"What sins?"

"Wait a minute," I said. "Are ya trying to pull a fast one?"

"No, what are ya talkin' about?"

"The 20 dollars I lent you last week?"

She swallowed hard and turned pale. "I hope you're kidding me." I frowned. "What twenty?" she asked.

"Don't give me that. You know, the 20-dollar bill."

Disturbed, she said, "I don't remember."

"O my! I guess I'm not getting paid back, am I?"

Cringing, she said, "I didn't say that."

"OK then. Just give me your rosary, and we'll call it even."

"O no!" she shouted.

"Then, how about if I trade you my ruby rosary for yours, and I'll forget the twenty you owe me?"

"No way!"

Showing her the miraculous medal around my neck, another one I carry within my oil pack, and the one hanging on my key change at my side, I said, "What about if I give you these?"

"Wow! Our Lady hems you in; why so many?"

"Because I love her so much!"

"Naturally, she's your mother!"

"So it's a deal?"

"Never!"

"I'll give you a bite of my apple," I said, biting into one.

"Father, what's worse than finding a worm in your apple?"

"I don't know, what?"

"Finding a half of one," she said, laughing at me choking.

Clearing my throat, I said, "I'll give you another 20 dollars, too, for your rosary?"

"Come off it! Did Jeanne Jugan give up her rosary, or sell it to anyone?"

"No, of course not! She always clung to it, like you, Tessie."

"Well, then, you and no one else will ever have my crystal rosary and that's that! I'll just call home and see if my poor family can come up with your money. But don't lend me any more. You hear me, Father?" I nodded. "What did I want the twenty for anyway?"

"I don't remember," I said.

"Good Lord, you're as bad as me."

Aware of her fright, I ended my charade. "Tessie, Tessie, you don't owe me anything. I'm kidding you."

Her color returned. "Father, I thought you were going to take my rosary. You scared the devil outta me!"

"Good," I said. "That's my job!"

"And you do a good one."

Another day, with her rosary wrapped around her hands, she came up to me, saying, "Please pray, Father, that I don't become like poor Wanda; she doesn't know her own daughter."

"She's not that bad," I said. "She knows me."

"Everyone knows you, Father, your collar tips us off."

"You really think she doesn't know her own daughter?"

"Didn't you hear the story about her?"

"What story?"

"Not long ago, Wanda sat in her wheelchair near the front desk. Her daughter came right up to her face, saying, 'Do you know who I am?' Wanda looked her over twice, saying, 'Well no, I don't, but go right over there to the desk. They'll tell you who you are. They know everybody.' Her own daughter, Father, she didn't even know. Imagine that!"

"That's a fish story," I said, laughing at it.

"Just the same—fish stories tell the truth—you pray that I don't become like her."

"OK, but you pray that I remember," I said.

"Good God! You're worse than I am," she said. "What was it anyway that I asked you to pray for?"

"I don't remember."

"Good Lord!"

Every day, Tessie came up for Holy Communion with her crystal beads wrapped around her hands. One day, unsteady on her feet, she approached the sacrament. "Body of Christ," I said.

"Father, I'm dizzy," she responded.

Afraid that she might faint, I didn't give her the Eucharist. Instead, I took her arm to sit her down. "First, give me Him!" she demanded. Receiving the Lord, she sat down in the first pew. Near Tessie in the communion line, Sister Amez leaned over her and asked, "Tess, are you all right?"

"Now I am. I got Jesus!" she proclaimed and kissed the crucifix on her beads.

As Tessie became more feeble-minded, her faith grew stronger. Now she possessed three rosaries: one she wrapped around her leg, another she wore as a necklace, and the crystal one was always wrapped around her hands. She clutched that one for dear life. No one could take any of them from her. No one!

One day, I admired her rosary glittering in the sun. "My, what a beautiful rosary you have!" I said.

"Thanks, Father."

"May I see it," I asked, taking hold of it.

Not letting go, she said, "See with your eyes, not with your hands."

"Are you afraid I'll steal it?"

"No, I'm afraid you'll forget to give it back, and I'll forget I gave it to you. But here you can touch it and bless it," she said, gripping it tighter. After I blessed it, she kissed my hand and her glass beads, saying, "I just can't seem to pray it anymore. All I can do is hold it, but it feels like I'm holding our Blessed Mother's hand."

"Wow! You're a contemplative."

"What's that?"

"You're praying beyond words. I pray the whole rosary every day and I never experience holding our Lady's hand. You're special to pray like that."

"But I didn't even know I was praying."

"Wonderful! That's contemplation. How did you learn that kind of prayer?" I asked.

"I guess by the Holy Spirit. Often, when I'm holding my rosary, I sing the hymn *Spirit Of The Living God Fall Afresh On Me*. It's then that I feel the Blessed Mother's hand in mine," she said. "So I'm a … What am I again?"

"A contemplative."

"How about that!"

"Please, Tessie, pray for my special intention," I said.

"If I remember."

One evening, during our supper, a resident came to me, and said, "Father, Tessie swallowed her rosary beads."

"No way," I said.

"She did, Father."

"Her crystal ones?" I asked. He nodded. "How?"

"She swallowed it with her spaghetti."

"And you watched her?"

"Yeah, but I didn't think she'd do it." He knew I didn't believe him. "Go ask her," he said.

I sat down at the table. "Tessie, did you swallow your rosary?"

"Yes, Father," she said, dropping down her head.

"Were you afraid someone would steal it?"

"Of course not."

"Why then?"

"Because now I'll always have Jesus by my heart," she said with her hand on her chest.

I reported the incident to Sister Amez who brought her to the hospital. In the emergency unit, they took an X-ray. Sure enough, the crystal rosary showed up with the silver crucifix right near her heart. Like going fishing, the doctor hooked the chain rosary and pulled it up and out of her mouth. Sister told me the X-ray was framed and hung in the department of 'Our Lady of Radiology'. I laughed.

"It's true," she said, "except for the part of 'Our Lady of Radiology'."

In fear that she would swallow her rosary again, Sister Amez kept it. Tessie threatened to hire a lawyer if she didn't get it back. After she got deeply depressed over not having her beads, the psychiatrist ordered it returned to her, saying, "There are rosaries all over the place; if she wanted, she could swallow any one of them." When Sister Amez gave it back to her, Tessie closed her fist over it and beamed. She sparkled like a poor woman cupping a handful of diamonds.

For at least another year, Tessie's crystal rosary glittered around her hands. Then in the month of August, she became seriously sick. As I anointed her, I noticed her clutching a white rosary. After celebrating the Sacrament of the Sick, I asked, "Where's your crystal one?"

"Father, you know I've been sick and sleeping a lot." She yawned. "Not wanting it to disappear, I put it in a safe place."

"Where?" I asked.

"I forget," she said. "Isn't it awful?" Suddenly, she fell asleep. Hearing her snore, I cupped her face, kissed her good night, and whispered, "I love you."

That Saturday, the eighth of August, Tessie's hour had come. Her children, the Little Sisters, the aides, and I were praying the rosary around her bed. As we started the fourth glorious mystery, the 'Assumption of Mary', she stopped breathing, and we stopped praying.

One-by-one her seven children kissed their mother, whispering loving sentiments. Suddenly, as we were all leaving the room, she breathed again.

"Let's finish the rosary," Mother Vincent said.

As we finished the rosary and made the sign of the cross, Tessie breathed her last two breaths. In the stilled-silence, Sister Amez captured our attention by rolling down the blue blanket off Tessie's warm body. "Look!" she said.

In each hand, Tessie held a white rosary. It was the feast day of Saint Dominic, who instituted the celebrated rosary.

However, we never did find Tessie's *crystal rosary*.

***Blest are you among women
And blest is the fruit of your womb.***

—Luke 1:42

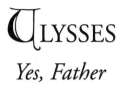ULYSSES

Yes, Father

Sitting on his bicycle in front of the Calvary statues, Ulysses wore his Yankees baseball cap, and around his neck outside his shirt, he wore a huge Miraculous Medal. Meeting him at the foot of the cross, I asked, "Ulysses, are you named after the general?"

"Yes," he said. "And my mother liked Grant's nickname. Do you know it, Father Christopher?"

"No, I don't, but call me Father Chris; I like it better," I said. "Tell me the general's nick name."

"Unconditional Surrender Grant," he said. "He got it at Fort Donelson. The enemy general defending the fort asked what terms Grant would give them. Ulysses replied, 'No terms other than an unconditional and immediate surrender can be accepted….'" Climbing onto his bicycle, he continued, "Mom liked the name 'Ulysses' but the general's nickname reminded her how we all should live."

"How?"

"Unconditional and immediate surrender to God on His terms."

"And why the big medal?"

Holding it with both hands, he said, "It reminds me to

surrender to God totally and completely like Mother Mary."

Pulling out my miraculous medal from underneath my shirt, I clutched it, and said, "Now my medal, too, will remind me to surrender like Mother Mary."

"That's the spirit, Father Chris," he said, riding off like a general on his war-horse.

One day, after the 11 o'clock Mass, Ulysses and I drove to Kelly Drive in the Fairmount section of the city. We parked behind the Art Museum near the falls and walked along the riverside. "Don't fall in," I said. "You might drown with that holy anchor around your neck."

"No, Father, it won't make me drown; it's my life preserver."

Feeling it, I said, "It's not real metal; it's plastic."

"But it's a real medal," he said. "It anchors me in heaven."

After walking about a mile, we stopped at Grant's Monument. Sitting down on a park bench near the statue of the general on his horse, Ulysses, told me this story:

"Once upon a time," he began, "a lady died and saw herself at the pearly gates. She rang the bell chimes. Saint Peter appeared sticking his head through the bars, asking, 'May I help you?'

'I want to come in,' she said.

'Do you know the passwords?' Peter asked.

The woman thought ... 'Jesus is Lord!'

'Yes, He is, but that's not it.'

'Jesus is the Resurrection and the Life?'

'Certainly, but they aren't the words either.'

'God so loved the world that—'

'No again.'

'Listen, Pete,' the frustrated woman said, 'Jesus has prepared a place for me in there so you better let me in.'

'As soon as you give me the passwords, darling.'

'Lord, save me!'

'Sorry, try again.'

Now annoyed, she shouted, '*I give up!*'

Heaven's gate swung wide. 'Come on in,' invited the gatekeeper."

"OK, I like it," I said. "I'll use that story in a homily someday."

"Good," he said, "you can also mention Mother Mary's three-step surrender program."

"Which is?"

"I can't do it. He can do it. I'll let Him do it."

"Now, I have a ready-made sermon in my heart on unconditional surrender," I said. "I just gotta preach it."

Back near the Art Museum, we admired a Greek sculpture. "What do you see?" he asked.

"I see the naked Zeus," I answered, "holding his naked son. With one hand, the little boy is trying to reach his father's neck; but he can't, because the other hand clutches a piece of garment that prevents him from embracing his father. However, I see their eyes focused on one another." Looking at Ulysses, I said, "And what do you see?"

"I see God the Father and myself as the little boy. I see the garment as a symbol of the world." He took a deep breath, looked into my eyes, and continued, "This artwork reflects my desire for God, but it also reflects my desire for the world. I want both, but I can't have both. I must let go of one to have the other." He pointed to Zeus. "I see the Father's eyes speaking to me as if to say, 'Son, let go of the passing world so you can wrap your arms around Me.' Ulysses looked at me and asked, "What does it mean to you?"

Thinking about Job, I focused on Ulysses' blue eyes and answered, "To me it means that naked I came forth from God and naked I shall return."

"Amen," he said.

The next few months, Ulysses appeared always tired. The doctor said he was anemic, and prescribed iron supplements. Unable to ride his bicycle anymore, he gave it to me along with his Yankees cap containing an apple in it. That summer he suffered a heart attack and found out that he had terminal cancer. In his hospital room, I asked, "Ulysses, how are you?"

"Miserable! Father, it's not fair! I'm only 67. I came to Holy Family Home to retire, not to die. I was fine before I came here. Why me? Why did I suffer a heart attack? Why do I have cancer? Why am I dying? Why did I come here? Why, Father, why?"

I wanted to say, "Grab hold of your life preserver and surrender like Mother Mary", but I dared not. He was too angry. Instead, I said, "Only God knows."

"Father Chris, since you can't answer any of my questions, can you make your visit short, and I'll ask God myself," he said in a rage.

"OK, but don't expect any answers," I said, becoming upset with his anger, although I understood his fear. I, too, feared death.

A short time later, Ulysses came back to us from the hospital to die. Seeing him in his room, I asked, "Well, did God answer your questions?"

"No, He didn't, Father, but He did change my night into day."

"Really, how?" I asked, happy to see him not angry.

"Well, after you left me in the hospital, I pointed my rage—both barrels—at God. I'll be like Moses, I thought, and climb Mount Sinai and demand answers from the Almighty One.

Dozing off, after invoking the Holy Spirit and holding my medal, I had a dream:"

> *As a boy, I was climbing a rugged mountain with an angel ahead of me. When dusk became night, my angelic guide faded from my sight. Almost to the top, all alone, I sat next to a rock. Down below I saw human shadows, representing my ugly gremlins: pain and suffering, fear and guilt, anger and depression. They were all there lurking to devour me.*
>
> *Suddenly, I saw flashes of ragged lightning and heard clashes of booming-rolling thunder. Close to me, lightning struck a tree, splitting it in two and blazing it with golden fire. Both the mountain and my body shook. I urinated in my pants. Now only one question really mattered. Grasping my Miraculous Medal with both hands and with all my might, I shouted, "O God, where are You?"*
>
> *From the burning tree, I heard a gentle voice. "Fear not, Ulysses, look beside you."*
>
> *Bowing my head, I said, "Yes, Father."*
>
> *Turning around to look at the rock beside me, I saw Jesus instead, glowing in the divine firelight and tongues of fire surrounding me. He wore black clothes and a white collar, like you Father. "Surrender," He said, "like my mother."*
>
> *Letting go of my medal, I threw up my youthful hands, saying, "I give up!" The fire burned out, and it became pitch black. Blinded, I reached for the Lord and hugged Him in my childhood. Releasing my embrace, I grabbed hold of His black belt, and He pulled me up to the top of the mountain. When night faded into day, he vanished. On my young person—I couldn't believe my eyes—I saw and felt the five*

wounds of Christ. He said from within my heart, "Come!"
    "Where?" I asked.
    "Home," He answered.

"Father, what do you think?"

Envious of his dream, I answered his question, saying, "Like Job, I would put my hand on my mouth and ask no more questions."

"Yes, Father," he said. "Father ..."

"Yes, Ulysses."

"How blessed we are with you!" His face beamed. "Other people around the world are not so fortunate. I heard that many poor souls pack lunches, walk miles, and even sleep under trees—in all kinds of weather—to find a priest for the supernatural sacraments that bring us heaven on earth. And here we are living in the same home with a priest. I thank God for you." Tears ran down his cheeks. "And I thank God for the Little Sisters of the Poor who care for us, because without them we wouldn't have our Holy Family Home, nor the chapel, the tabernacle, the Most Blessed Sacrament, or you."

"Don't I know it, Ulysses, how true it is!"

Six weeks later, on the Feast of the Annunciation, Ulysses left us while the aides and Sister Amez were changing his *wet* pajama pants. Dying naked, except for the Miraculous Medal around his neck and in his hands, he surrendered himself, unconditionally and immediately, to God on His terms.

Standing next to Sister Amez, I blessed his body and said, "Another graduate."

"*Summa Cum Laude*," she whispered.

At the funeral Mass, I preached my ready-made homily,

*'**Surrender**,'* the one Ulysses had tucked into my heart along with Mother Mary's three-step program.

The epitaph on his tombstone simply read:

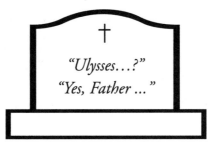

Father, into your hands I commend my spirit.

—Luke 23:46

VERA

The Lord's Merciful Pest

Merciful Sister Vera, Little Sister of the Poor and one of our oldest residents, took the greatest pleasure in little things. While she radiated the joy of the Lord and sang his mercies, she also could test others' patience—but not mine. On the contrary, she amused me so. On one occasion, she pushed her wheelchair down the corridor to my apartment, banging the walls all the way. Gently, as with a feather, she knocked.

As I opened the door, she stood bouncing her index finger off her pursed lips. "Shh, Father Chris, I've come to shine your shoes," she said. "Don't tell anybody."

"No, not a soul," I said, zippering my lips. "Come in."

"Got any coffee?"

"Sure, and cream donuts, too."

"Wonderful!"

Holding the Divine Mercy holy card, she plopped in her wheelchair and placed the holy image on her lap. Her shaky hands took the coffee and donut from me, saying, "God's so good! Isn't He, Father?"

"Indeed!" I exclaimed.

Blowing away the steam, she sipped the hot beverage. "And

so merciful, too!" When she bit the donut, sugar powder snowed down onto the divine image and over her black, winter habit. "Oops!" She smiled, licked the card, kissed it, and said, "My Jesus, how sweet thou art!"

Taking an apple, I cut out the core and put peanut butter in its place, saying, "Why can't God make apples without cores?"

"He could, Father, if He wanted. After all, he made Coors Beer without the cores."

Laughing, I said, "He sure did!"

"Father, can beer make you smarter?"

"No."

"Well, it made Bud *wiser*," she said, grinning at my frown.

"But, what about the shine?"

Looking down at my scuffed shoes, she answered, "O Father, they're already shiny. You don't need a shine. They're fine."

"I can see that," I said.

After enjoying her treat, she asked for my blessing. As she made the sign of the cross, she said, "Remember now, loose lips sink ships."

"Mum's the word," I said, zippering my lips.

Out in the hallway stood Sister Amez. With her hands on her hips, she asked, "Sister Vera, why are you bothering Father Chris?"

Smiling, she answered, "I just stopped for the chaplain's blessing. Since you're here, you should get one, too. Better yet, make it a confession; it'll do your soul good." Pushing her wheelchair, she clanged her way back through the corridor.

Grinning at me, Sister Amez said, "Sorry, Father, Sister can be a pest at times. Just tell her how busy you are, and she won't bother you, I hope."

"She's not a bother," I said. "She's a blessing."

Soon after, Sister Vera visited Mary, one of the cantankerous residents. Meeting them, I said, "Good morning. How's—"

"You're the one I want, not her!" Mary shouted. Sitting in her wheelchair, Sister chattered away as Mary squirmed in her bed. Mary yelled again, "Please, shut yer mouth while I talk to the priest, will *ya*?"

Sister looked at me, smiled, and said, "Father, isn't she so sweet. God love her."

Mary fumed even more. "I had it with ya. Git outta here!"

"Father, isn't she a darling?"

"I'll darling ya!" Mary screamed. Looking at me, she pleaded, "Please, shut her up!"

"O how I love the old people," Sister said.

"For crying out loud, will ya shut yer big trap!" Mary raged.

To prevent Mary from going into cardiac arrest, I placed my hands on the back of Sister's chair to wheel her away. Seeing this, Mary said, "That's right, take her home and put her to bed—that one needs a long nap."

"Make sure you get your nap too, sweetheart," Sister said over her grin.

Mary pointed her pretended loaded finger at Sister, saying, "O yeah, I'll kill you dead!" Cocking her thumb back, she blurted out, "Bang! Take that, darling."

"Bye, sweetie," Sister said.

"Yeah, yeah, git goin' before I sweeten ya real good, honey," she said, flapping her hand, like shooing away an irritating fly. Outside the door, I heard Mary sigh, "Thank God, I thought she'd never leave!"

Impressed with Sister's Christ-like attitude, I asked her, "How could you be so nice to so much ridicule?"

"O Father, she doesn't know what's she doing. She's only a child." Laughing, she added, "The old people amuse me so, and

God is so merciful to them."

"I know it," I said. "He shows His mercy through you."

"You're a holy priest, Father Chris."

"O Sister, no I'm not. Sometimes I'm like Mary and I don't know what I'm doing either."

"Don't worry, Father, in His great mercy He forgives you, too."

"How do you know?" I asked, curious about her answer.

"Behold the crucifix, Father: 1 cross + 3 nails = 4-given," she said, numbering her fingers.

Once in the chapel, I saw her walk a few unsteady steps and place flowers in front of the Divine Mercy painting. Sneaking up behind her, I whispered, "Pray for me, Sister Vera; I still don't know what I'm doing."

"I always pray for you, Father." Looking at the painting, she whispered to Jesus, saying, "O Jesus, have mercy on Father Chris; he still doesn't know what he's doing."

She shuffled back to her wheelchair, pulled out a leaflet of the Divine Mercy from her bag of prayers, and gave it to me. "Go into the office and make me fifty copies, but keep quiet about it," she said, bouncing the index finger off her pursed lips.

"Loose lips sink ships," I whispered, zippering my lips.

Flicking her finger at me, she nodded and said, "Hurry now. I'll be waiting."

In the office, I ran off the fifty copies. Noticing the printouts, Patricia Hai, the office manager, said, "For Sister Vera?"

"My lips are sealed," I said.

"That's the second batch today."

"Wow! I wish I could promote the Lord like her."

"Me, too!" Pat exclaimed.

Back in the chapel, she took the fifty copies, counted out ten, and gave them to me, saying, "Father, pass these out for our dear Lord. Tell His people His mercies are beyond counting, but don't let anyone know they came from me; they might think I'm a pest."

"So," I said. "You're the Lord's Pest."

"That's right, Father, and God be merciful to us sinners."

On Holy Thursday evening, after celebrating the Mass of the Lord's Supper at our home, I sat in the chapel before the radiant repository of the Blessed Sacrament, sensing His Real Presence. A beautiful feeling came over me, and I desired to spend the night in Eucharistic adoration and thank God for my priesthood. Also, I expected something wonderful to happen. I might fall asleep, I thought, like the apostles, and perhaps have my divine dream. I intended to "pitch my tent" and stay the night with the Lord. Just then, my beeper vibrated against my hip. "Now what?" I whispered under my breath. At the front desk, I asked the busy operator, "Did you beep me?"

"Yes, Father, Sister Vera took sick." I flew up the stairwell and entered Sister's room.

"She's barely breathing," Sister Amez said. One-by-one, the Little Sisters arrived. Here we go again, I thought, facing that ugly 'Grim Reaper' on this holy night. Taking my newly consecrated oil which came from the Chrism Mass that morning, I anointed Sister Vera. Suddenly she revived, looked at me, and asked me, "Got any coffee?"

Restrained laughter erupted, and then the Sisters returned to their duties. Sister Amez asked, "Father, can you go to Dunkin' Donuts for some coffee and vanilla cream donuts for our sick Little Sister?"

"OK, I'm on my way!"

When I returned with the coffee, I said to Sister Amez, "Mum's the word."

Sitting up in bed, Sister Vera said, "O Father, she won't tell. Give me my coffee." Sister Amez left us alone. After sipping her warm drink, she asked me, "Is coffee a medicine?"

"I don't think so."

"Well, it made Max**well**."

Laughing at her joke, I said, "Here's your donut."

"Thank you, Father, and thank you God for all your gifts, especially for your priesthood and Holy Eucharist."

"Amen!" I proclaimed.

After our treat, Sister fell asleep, and I decided to sit at her side and pray the rosary for her. At the end of it, she became agitated in her sleep, squirming in her bed. With the eyes of faith, I could see Jesus Christ crucified in her.

On Good Friday, the Little Sisters invited me back to her room for Morning Prayer. Entering, I saw two burning candles on the little altar for the dying. Like a fish out of water, Sister flipped-flopped in her bed. After our prayers, I anointed her thinking that maybe she would die at the 3 o'clock hour of mercy, but she didn't. At dusk, she became still. She looked like she was in her casket. A crucifix rested on her chest with her four written vows under her garment: poverty, chastity, obedience and hospitality. Death was moving closer, I knew.

On Holy Saturday Sister Amez had a hard time getting her pulse, and I couldn't see her breathing. "How do you know she's still living?" I asked.

"Father, it's like in chapel this morning. Didn't you feel the absence of the Real Presence when you looked into the empty tabernacle?"

"I did."

"It'll be like that. When He takes her, you'll know she's gone."

"I'm not so sure that I'll know; that's your charism," I said.

"Wouldn't it be a blessing, Sister, if she died on Easter Sunday?"

"Sure, but that's up to God, and you can't second guess Him; although you might make Him laugh at your theological hunch."

Holy Saturday afternoon, we were once again gathered around Sister Vera. Again, I anointed her. "Through this holy anointing may God in His love and *mercy* help you with the grace of the Holy Spirit.

"Amen," the Sisters responded.

"May the Lord who frees you from sin save you and raise you up."

"Amen."

Afterward, we prayed the rosary. At the three o'clock hour we began the Chaplet of Divine Mercy. During the devotion, Sister started gasping. She opened her eyes—we halted our prayers. She twisted from side-to-side, pushed herself up on the pillow, and fixated all aglow at the upper corner of the room. In the holy hush, we heard Sister Vera utter her last prayerful words, "O Mother Mary! O Jesus, mercy!" She gasped and fell back.

Placing my hands on hers, I could no longer feel her presence; instead, I felt His. As for me, I could only see Jesus Christ crucified in her. Before praying for the dead, I waited a while, just in case she breathed again. "It's time," I said to myself. Bending over, I kissed her forehead, praying. "Eternal rest grant to Sister Vera, O Lord—" She gasped two more breaths. We held ours...

"And may the souls of the faithful departed, through the mercy of God rest in peace," Sister Amez prayed.

"Amen!" we responded.

"She's having coffee and donuts with Jesus in heaven," Mother Vincent whispered, making us smile. Then we finished the Chaplet of Divine Mercy for dear Sister Vera, *the Lord's Merciful Pest.*

> **Blest are they who show mercy;**
> **mercy shall be theirs.**

—Matthew 5:7

WENDY
A Big Teddy Bear

Carefully, she waved her cane, saying, "Father, got a moment?"

"Anything for you, Wendy."

"You're OK, Father. I don't care what they say about you," she jested.

"Let's go on the patio," I suggested. "We'll talk there."

"OK, Father. OK."

We sat down under the umbrella table. "I've been wondering how's your street ministry at Saint Gabriel's doing?"

"OK. It's in God's hands."

"We really enjoyed our visit there last week. I love the name you gave it, *Our House*. And those cheese steaks—out of this world!"

"They were Pat's Steaks; I'm glad you enjoyed it all."

"O I did. You should write a book about your street ministry."

"But first I have to finish *Heaven's Homecoming*. I don't think I'll live that long to write a second book."

"Really, I can't believe you'll still writing that one; it seems like you started it years ago."

"I did, but I need more characters. Would you like to be one?"

"Me? I'm flattered."

"Well, there IS one qualification."

"What?"

"Ya gotta die first."

"Good heavens! Don't be in any hurry for my act. I'm not ready for death yet."

"Neither am I, nor am I ready to lose you, my inspiration."

"OK, Father, OK. By the way, I wrote this for you." She handed me her poem.

OUR HOUSE

Not a stately mansion
Where famous people come to play.
No, just a simple little row house
Where weary people come and pray.
Just knock and you'll meet our Father OK
With his friendly jokes and boyish play.
He'll shake your hand and then he'll say:
"Come on in, rest, and let us pray!"

"Wendy, it's great! I'll frame it and hang it in Our House," I said. "You are my inspiration."

"And you're my Father OK."

During one of our religion classes, I spoke about meditation and the gift of the imagination. At the end of the session, I gave my teaching-students homework, saying to them, "Tonight, before you go to sleep, meditate by imagining yourself as a child in the arms of God the Father and just let Him love you."

After class Wendy said, "But Father, I'm afraid of God."

"Why?" I asked.

"My fear stems from my first grade teacher. Sister Clare likened Him to Santa Claus, you know, 'You better watch out, you better not cry, you better not pout, I'm telling you why, God is coming to town,' she recited and glared. 'He sees you when you're sleeping; He knows when you're awake; He knows when you are bad or good, so be good—or else.' I believed then and now that I got a scolding, a spanking, and a bag of coal coming to me for my past sins."

"O Wendy, God doesn't scold and spank; He hugs and kisses," I said, delighting her. "Just do your homework and see what happens." As we parted company, I became concerned, though, over my own sins and death.

The next morning, Wendy tapped on my door with the handle of her cane. Nodding to her, I smiled and said, "Come on in, rest a while, and let us pray."

"OK, Father. OK. How are you?"

"O Wendy, I don't think I'm meant long for this world."

"For goodness sake, you better not die before me, because I need you to lead me to the gates of heaven. Besides, I want you to celebrate my 'graduation ceremony.'"

"What do you mean?"

"My funeral Mass, of course."

"It will be my honor."

"We sat down at my table. "O my, I actually met God the Father and God the Son." Tears ran down her cheeks. "All these years I was afraid to meet God. I never knew Jesus as my real brother and Himself as my very own Father—until I did my homework last night."

"Tell me about it," I said.

"Father, I imagined myself as a child in the loving arms of Father God; and for extra credit, I tried to see myself sitting on

His lap. Then, with my rosary in my hands, I must have fallen asleep, dreaming:"

Mysteriously, I found myself as a little girl, standing on a stone bridge above a waterfall with my guardian angel. Looking down, I saw the boy Jesus, sitting on a wooden bridge with His bare feet hanging over a brook. He waved and said, 'Come to me.'

Climbing down with my angel through the fragrant flowers and green grass, I met Him at the bank of the babbling brook. His brown hair and eyes resembled His brown clothes. All excited, He pointed up over the stone bridge to a radiant rainbow.

Then, out of the majestic colors, Father God appeared, soaring down on a white horse with jumbo jet wings. Landing in front of us, He said, 'Whoa, Regal!'

'Come, my sister,' Jesus said as my angel disappeared. Reaching down, the Father hoisted and mounted us with Him.

'Giddy up,' He said, tapping His gentle beast with His black boots. Over the rainbow we flew. He wore loose clothing with His red sleeves rolled up to His elbows. His white beard and hair fluttered in the air. Gliding down—in the thrill of it all—we skimmed the snowcapped mountains and the evergreen trees. Beyond the verdant valley, we skidded across the blue ocean, landing back at the garden brook.

Sliding off Regal, I exclaimed, 'Gee whiz, Jesus, you got a wonderful Daddy!'

'Wendy, my sister, He's OUR Daddy,' Jesus whispered in my ear. And when you pray say, 'Our Father'.'

Peeking at the Almighty One, I asked, 'Are you really my daddy, too?'

'You better believe it, my little girl,' He said, springing off His high horse.

'Daddy, Daddy,' I cried, lifting up my hands and heart to Him. All excited—more than over the sky-adventure— He picked me up, swung me around in His jolly laugh, and carried me to the wooden bridge. He plucked a lily, gave it to me, and sat me on His lap. As I sniffed the flower, I fingered His white beard to feel the really real. He embraced me within His gentle arms and sang a love song in my ear:

You're daddy's little girl to have and hold,
You're sugar, you're spice, and you're everything nice,
And you're daddy's little girl.

In the joy of God the Son, God the Father carried me back to the bank of the brook through the fragrant garden, kissing and hugging me all the way there in the spray of the waterfall. Before He put me down, I hugged Him as my very own big teddy bear. Joyfully, He mounted Regal. When I reached up to go with Him, my dream ended.

"Wow wee, Wendy! And your past sins were never mentioned in your dream?"

"Never, Father OK."

"Good for you. I'm giving you an A+ for your homework assignment and another plus for your extra credit work. Your total grade: A++. Excellent! I'm happy for you. I really wish I could dream like you." Standing up, I kissed her and saw her out, saying, "Darling, you pick me up when I'm down."

The next time I saw her, she handed me another poem, saying, "You inspired this one, too."

WENDY'S PRAYER

I am old now, O Lord.
My days left on earth are few.
And please dear Daddy God,
Let me spend them all
On Your lap, loving You.

"Wendy, how do you write such wonderful poems?"

"If they're wonderful, it's the Holy Spirit who inspires me and prompts me to write and write until it's right."

One Sunday after Mass, Sister Amez met me, saying, "Wendy fainted in the chapel during her morning prayers. She's in bed. Please, come and anoint her. You never know."

When I got to her room, I greeted Wendy and her visitors. For a while, we all talked about the rainy season. Then Wendy suddenly interrupted the weather report.

"OK Father, let us pray." After I ministered the Sacrament of the Sick, she said, "O Father, please come back and hear my confession, OK?"

"OK! For you, Wendy, anything."

That evening I met Wendy again. She asked, "Did the anointing today absolve me from my sins?"

"Yes, it did."

"Good, but I still want a confession."

"OK, what are your sins?"

"I can't remember any sins; I just want more blessings."

"OK," I said, hearing her sinless confession.

"Now, Father OK, I'm OK, too. I think you better get my eulogy ready, and if you please, fit me into your book," she said. "Would you believe it, I'm not afraid to die anymore because even though I walk in the dark valley I fear no evil for I am His little girl."

Believing that her days on earth were few, I asked, "May I copy your poems?"

"OK, but I don't think they're worth copying."

"They inspired me."

"And you always inspire me," she said, yawning herself to sleep. Not wanting to leave her, I stood at the doorway watching my sleeping beauty praying in her sleep. Over and over, she moaned, "Our Father ... Our Father ... Our Father ..."

Stepping back to her bedside, I leaned over, kissed her forehead, and whispered, "Rest now, Daddy's little girl. Let Him have you and hold you, because you're sugar and spice and everything nice."

Before going to bed that night, I stopped to pray over Wendy again. She was still sleeping and moaning, "Our Father ... Our Father ... Our Father."

The morning after, to our shock, Wendy's body was found half-in and half-out of bed. Her arms were stretched out, looking like she was trying to go with someone somewhere. Around her neck, she wore her rosary, and on the floor by her feet was a holy card—an image of God the Father. Her countenance shone a glow of excitement. To prepare her eulogy, I read all her poems. The last one in her binder touched me the most and humbled me real good.

HEAVEN'S GATES

When I was young and fair,
Many times of going to heaven,
I did despair!

And then, I had a dream,
At heaven's gates, myself,
I did find!

A blinding light shone on my face
And God did me embrace,
As I heard Him say:
"So you're a friend of Father OK.
OK, then, come on in,
And forever stay."

Although, I still feared death, Wendy would always be to me an inspiration to write and a special reminder that God, the Father, is *A Big Teddy Bear.*

> ***This is how you are to pray:***
> ***'Our Father....'***

—Matthew 6:9

XAVIER ANTHONY

A Hush of Divine Awe

Keeping my appointment, I first met Brother Xavier Anthony in the sacristy before Mass. After our greeting, I remarked, "So you're a Franciscan?"

"Yes, indeed. I'm an OFM and a FBI—Order of Fat Men and Foreign Born Irish."

"Wonderful!" I said, not sure of what to make of him. Admiring his religious garb, though, I asked, "Brother, how many habits do you have?"

He answered, "One good one; the rest are bad."

I chuckled. "So what's the good one?"

"You're looking at it," he said, "Me in my brown habit serving you at Mass."

"Brother, you're the best." Wanting to know more about him, I asked, "So you weren't born in Ireland?"

"No, but my mother was," he said.

"Where?" I inquired.

"Top of the bottle."

"Where's that, Brother?"

"Cork," he answered, and I laughed. "And what about you, Father?"

"Right here in good 'ol Philadelphia, but my great-grand-parents were born in Donegal where they eat the skins and all." His Irish eyes smiled even though he had heard the saying many times.

"We'll get along fine," he said. "Laughter is the beginning of prayer."

"OK then, let us pray," I said, vesting myself for Mass.

Brother often quoted his founder, Saint Francis. "Everything in man should halt in awe. Let all the world quake and let heaven exult when Christ the Son of the living God is there on the altar."

"OK, then, Brother, lead me to the altar," I would say, following him out of the sacristy.

One year, during Holy week, I got the flu. Doctor Ron, my physician, prescribed some antibiotics. For that week I stayed in bed with the sweats and chills. Everyday, except Holy Thursday, Brother visited me in my agony. On Spy Wednesday, I told him, "Brother, I'm not long for this world."

"I'll call the undertaker," he said, trying to humor me. "When he asks what you died from, I'll tell him, 'Nothing serious.'"

"Brother," I responded weakly, "make sure he sees to it that my epitaph reads, 'Now do you believe I was sick?'" He laughed and I moaned. "I'm not trying to be funny, Brother."

"You ARE sick!" he said, seriously.

Wondering if he knew something that I didn't know, I asked, "How do you know?"

"Because, Father Chris, you're out of character," he said, pointing his finger.

"Look at your hand, Brother … Three fingers point at yourself. It's easy to judge me; you're not the one sick."

"We're all sick, Father, and dying from original sin."

"Thank you, Brother Theologian!"

"You're welcome."

"Brother, you bother the heaven out of me."

"Is it I who bothers, Father, or rather you?"

I knew it was I. But to my shame, I was too proud to admit it then and there. I must have upset his Holy Thursday, too, because he didn't visit me with Holy Communion that cloudy day. Being sick in spirit now, I was sorrowful for bothering the heaven out of him. On Good Friday, my birthday, I felt even worse and became preoccupied with death. Brother brought me three presents. The first was a bright red apple.

"I never refuse an apple," I groaned.

"I hope it keeps the undertaker away," he said, hoping to humor me this time.

Mustering a Christian smile, I said, "You mean the doctor, I hope."

The second gift was a ceramic crucifix. The good Brother hung it on the wall in front of me. Now I had one in front of me and one behind me above my bed. Sister Death howled off the walls, echoing in my mind.

The third gift, the best of all, was Holy Communion. As I realized His Real Presence, peace entered my soul. "Thank you, Brother," I said. "I'm sorry about Wednesday; please forgive me." Accepting my apology, he began the prayers. As I received Our Lord, I felt health in my sickness; joy in my sorrow, and pleasure in my pain. He finished the prayers by giving me his Irish Blessing:

> *I wish you health, and I wish you wealth*
> *And I wish you gold in store.*
> *I wish you heaven after this life,*
> *And how can I wish you more?*

"Happy Birthday, Father!"

"Thanks again, Brother, pray for my birthday wish."

After my recovery, we became like brothers, and he began assisting me in my street ministry, teaching me about Saint Francis. One evening, when we were coming home from Mass at *Our House*, Brother said, "Let's go preach in the marketplace."

Feeling intimidated, I said, "Brother Xavier Anthony, I don't think so. You don't know this neighborhood. There's a mix religion and race. Some are Muslims, and some are addicts. We could be stabbed, shot, killed, or worse," I said, fearing for my life. "Besides, I wouldn't know what to say."

"Then say nothing," Brother said. "Just follow the wisdom of Saint Francis."

"And what's that?"

"At all times preach the Gospel, and when necessary use words," he said, quoting his founder.

"OK, then, we'll go, but keep a holy quiet."

"I won't say a word," he said, telling me this Franciscan story:

"One day Saint Francis said to Brother Leo, 'Let's go into the marketplace and preach.' Wearing their habits they walked all through the market.

'When will we preach?' Leo asked.

'We just did', Francis answered."

"That's a good story," I said. "We'll just walk through the market in our witness clothes and let God do the preaching."

In the market, Brother got us some ice cream to go. I could feel the eyes staring. Only God knew what the people were thinking. Brother's habit drew more attention than my Roman collar. One customer eyed Brother up and down, finally asking him, "Are ya a Monsignor?"

"No, he's not," I answered, "but I am a priest."

"O that's good… Will you pray, priest, for peace in our streets?"

"OK," I responded, "and God bless you."

Outside, we had to pass through a rowdy group of young people in the parking lot. I could smell the marijuana. I heard one of them say, "Put it away; they're men of God."

Whispering to Brother, I said, "Pray."

Another one of them stopped us. He had a cast on his arm and cuts on his face. Despite his ailments, he beamed, asking Brother, "Can you bless us?"

"No, he can't. He's not a priest, but I can," I said. "I'm Father Chris and the silent one is Brother Xavier Anthony." As I blessed them, they bowed their heads. After the blessing, they thanked us and shook our hands. My Franciscan companion never said a word, but God preached a moving sermon that night through my Roman collar and Brother's "one good habit."

When we got back to the tranquility of Holy Family Home, we sat on a swing built for two, surrounded by a wall in the brightly lit garden. Face-to-face we swung savoring our ice cream. Between one of his chocolate scoops, Brother commented, "I'm glad we don't have to live 'out there' in all that tension and violence."

"Yeah," I responded. "And I'm glad we live 'in here' in all this calm and peace, thanks to the Little Sisters," I said, enjoying the ice cream. "Do you know Brother that I wrote a poem about 'out there and in here' while sitting on this very swing? I have it memorized. Would you like to hear it?"

Still giving his tongue a sleigh ride, he nodded.

Handing over my ice cream to him, I guided my hands around the garden. With Wendy in mind, my inspirational poet, I quoted:

OUR LITTLE PATCH OF GREEN

In my little patch of green,
Surrounded by a wall,
I sit in a swing made for two,
In a world of so much awe.

Outside, tires are screeching,
Sirens blaring, lights flashing,
And people screaming,
All around my little patch of green.

But inside, butterflies are fluttering,
Among His sunlit flowers,
Squirrels scampering
Across His brilliant lawn,
And birds chirping
Above His glittering fountains,
All within my little patch of green.

Now as I sit in my prayer for peace,
My Good Shepherd grins,
And He swings me with Him,
In *our* little patch of green.

"Well done good and faithful servant," Brother said, finishing up all the ice cream, including mine, and swinging me with him in our little patch of green.

During religion class while I was teaching about prayer with Sister Amez, the good brown robe Franciscan Brother raised his hand, asking, "May I share a favorite prayer of our founder that pierces the heavens?"

"OK," I said. "Share it; we're all ears."

"It's powerful! It conquers all temptations, sin, and even death. Are you all ready to memorize it?"

"Speak the holy prayer," Sister Amez answered, as I held my pen, ready to write it down.

Moistening his lips with his tongue to show the sweetness of the prayer, he bowed his head, and just said, *"Jesus."* We waited for the rest of the prayer.

"That's it?" I finally asked.

"That's it."

Sister Amez said, "Brother, please repeat it. And slow down this time. You went to fast."

"Jesus," he whispered, closing his eyes and piercing the heavens. "It saves us from all the bad. Got it, Sister?"

"It's memorized," she said.

One evening while praying the Angelus before supper, Brother started babbling the words incoherently. Because he wasn't making any sense, he was taken to the hospital for a few days. They found out that he had low platelets. After receiving a blood transfusion, Brother started to feel better. I brought him Holy Communion each morning. After blessing him, I prayed our favorite prayer, *"Jesus"*.

For at least another year, Brother continued to serve me at the altars of Holy Family Home and *Our House* Ministries. On the feast of Corpus Christi, however, he served his last Mass at our home. At the sign of peace, I noticed that he didn't look well. Shaking his hand, I asked, "Are you OK?"

"I feel weak," he said. "But I'll be all right."

At communion time, I said, "Body of Christ."

"Jesus," he whispered. Bowing his head, he received. Seeing him losing color, though, I sat him down and dashed into the sacristy for a glass of water. When I came out, he was slumped down. Sister Amez and another nurse rushed up. They laid him on the floor and placed the seat cushion under his head. He bled from the nose and foamed at the mouth.

"He's going," Sister Amez whispered.

Quickly, I knelt down and anointed the good Brother. As I crossed his palms with holy oil, he took two last breaths, dying at the foot of the altar where he had served as my faithful servant, but God's first. His death made me fearful about my own; however, in the spotlight of the sanctuary, there was *a hush of divine awe.*

Be still and know that I am God.

—Psalm 46:10

YOEY

The Kiss of the Big Wow

Adorable Yoey, living in a urine-soaked bed, came to us sickly from her lonely, dilapidated, and rat-infested house. The Little Sisters who visited her on Good Friday morning said that the bad odors were unbearable. The compassionate ones wrapped her up in a blanket—breathing in the sweet fragrance of the suffering Christ—and transported her to our home.

After cutting the tangled knots from her hair, the Sisters and their aides showered her, manicured her nails, and gave her a prolonged bubble bath, shampooing her head. Setting her hair and perfuming her body, the wonder workers dressed her in new clothes. Like a queen on her throne, Yoey ate her first dinner at Holy Family Home. On Easter Sunday morning, I met her. All dressed up in her bonnet, she asked, "Yo, Fadder, is this heaven?"

"No, Yoey," I said. "It's almost heaven, but not quite."

"Well, it's heaven to me," she said.

In a few weeks, Yoey gained her strength and volunteered for all the activities, especially working the Flea Market, and in particular, handing out the church bulletins. One time, in the tea room, I held a cup of apple slices behind my back.

"Yoey," I said, "close your eyes and open your mouth, and I

will fill it with a big surprise."

Doing so, she exclaimed, "Yo!" Savoring the fruit, she added, "Again! Again!" As she opened her mouth and closed her eyes a second time, I pitched in another slice.

"Jesus, Mary, and Joseph, it tastes great!"

Handing her the rest, I said, "Here, share them with Jesus, Mary, and Joseph—they're the greatest!"

"Wow!" she said. "I like surprises."

One day at Mass, Yoey came up to receive Holy Communion.

"Body of Christ," I said.

"Amen," she responded. As she closed her eyes and opened her mouth, her false teeth came flying out to my total surprise. She just caught them in her hands, though, and laughed, "Yo, Fadder. These don't fit so good. Ya better be true to your teeth, or they'll be false to you." In His Eucharistic presence, I smiled. If she were embarrassed, she didn't show it. However, she never used those false teeth again.

Knowing how rarely Yoey got out, I once asked her, "Wanna go for a ride?"

"Yo, do I!"

Once we got outside our home, we drove under a fire hydrant's sprinkler and stopped. The shower and the sun made us see a double rainbow right in front of my car.

"Yo Fadder, look at that—Wow! It's even prettier than my rainbow painting on my wall," she said. "Make a wish; don't tell anybody or it won't come true." Closing our eyes, we made our wishes.

Going to *Wendy's* drive-thru for lunch, Christmas in July suddenly came to mind. Taking the tape of *Christmas with the Chipmunks*, I played: *All I Want For Christmas Is My Two Front Teeth.*

"Ha, that's my wish. All new teeth before Christmas!" she said, and then added. "O no, Fadder, I told my wish. Now it won't come true."

"Stop being superstitious," I said. "It's a sin."

"Fadder, what did you wish for?"

"I'm not telling."

"You can tell me," she persisted.

"Can you keep a secret?"

"I can."

"And so can I," I laughed.

After enjoying our burgers and fries, we drove home sipping our milkshakes and singing *Frosty the Snowman*. Back at the home, she asked me, "When we goin' again?"

"Soon," I said.

"I had fun, Fadder. My birthday is August 12th, ya know. I'll be 80. Don't forgit now, August 12th."

"Wow, 80!" I exclaimed. "You don't look 80." Blinking, she made pretty eyes at me. "You look more like 90!" Her toothless smile turned into a frown. "I mean 70."

Turning her frown upside down again, she asked, "So you'll take me out for my birthday?"

"And how!"

"Wow, you're my favorite priest!"

Everyday she proclaimed: "Yo, everybody, my birthday's comin' up. The 12th of August. I'll be 80. Fadder's takin' me out. My birthday's comin' up."

I would always kid her in front of everyone, saying, "Now, does Yoey look like she'll be 80?" They admired her looks. Then, I would say, "More like 90, right?"

"Yo Fadder, knock it off. You're crazy."

"I mean 70."

One night I met Yoey sitting outside on the patio swing. "Yo Fadder, how ya doin'?"

"Well, I'm not long for this world."

"Yo, cut it out, will ya!"

"OK, but you never know."

"Wow, look!" she said, pointing at the crescent moon. I sat down and swung with her. "Don't it look like God's thumb nail sticking out?"

"Yeah, it's beautiful."

"And look at all the twinkling stars. Wow!"

"Yo Yoey, that's God winking at us."

Blinking her twinkling baby blues, she made divine eyes at me. "I'm telling ya," she said, pointing back up at the stars. "If that's the bottom of heaven—Jesus, Mary, and Joseph—what must the top look like?"

"I can't imagine, but Jesus, Mary, and Joseph know."

"Wow, Fadder, God is something else, ain't He?"

"And how. He's Grrreat!"

"Don't forgit my birthday," she said. "It's comin' up. You're my favorite priest, ya know!"

On August 12th, we all met in the social hall for Yoey's 80th birthday party. When she entered the hall, we shouted, "Surprise!" After gaping at us, tears ran down her cheeks. We all ate ice cream and cake, and then she opened her big gift—a VCR for her TV.

"Yo, wow!" she clamored.

Sister Amez said to her, "Doctor O'Farrell wants to see you tomorrow to fit you for your new teeth."

"Wow! Now, I'll have my own." (I wondered who had owned her last set.) As I thought about asking her, she broke out singing, "All I Want For Christmas Is My [New] Front Teeth."

After her solo, I said, "But, Yoey, there's a catch."

"What?"

"Doctor O'Farrell said ya gotta wait for your teeth until his old-gray-mare dies."

"Yo, you're crazy," she said. "When we goin' ta *Wendy's*?"

"After ya git your new teeth. Then I can show you off," I said. "I get the first kiss, right?"

With her toothless smile and pretty blue eyes, she said, "Jesus gits the first kiss, and you, my favorite priest, gits the second."

"Wow wee! I can't wait!"

When the dentist had her teeth ready, Yoey became deathly sick. She came back from the hospital to die. In her room, Sister Amez said, "Doctor O'Farrell got your new teeth. Do you want him to come and fit them in for you?"

"Not today, Sister. The old gray mare just ain't what she used to be; but I'm happy!" she proclaimed.

"Well," I said, "I'm still waiting for that second kiss from my favorite old-gray-mare."

"Yo Fadder, cut it out. Don't worry; ya'll git it! Tell 'im, Sister."

"Yo Fadder, ya'll git it!" Sister said, imitating her.

Three days later, I anointed Yoey. I asked Sister Amez to call me if there was any change. Two-thirty in the morning my phone rang.

"Come quickly!"

Rushing to her bedside, I squeezed my little Saint Joseph. I saw Yoey pushing herself up and staring at the rainbow picture across from her bed. She closed her eyes and opened her mouth. Her gaping reminded me of the apple slices that I dropped into her mouth and the happy expression she gave us at her surprise party. However, now she looked more surprised. Making the sign of the cross on her forehead, I prayed, "Jesus, Mary, and Joseph."

Somehow my heart knew His saving presence for her and her personal intercession for my rainbow wish. As she caught her last two breaths, her gape widened, and she died experiencing the Surprise of all surprises—seeing God, Himself, I believe, at the top of heaven.

Sister Amez brought back Yoey's new teeth. Fitting them in her mouth before the spreading of rigor mortis, she said, "Yo Father, now you can git yer kiss from our new graduate."

Noticing an angelic halo around her face and an expression of happiness on her lips, I figured that Jesus got the first kiss. Fearful of death, I pressed my lips on her new front teeth and got the second kiss. And, I do believe, the old-gray-mare got from God her place in heaven and, yo, *the kiss of the big wow.*

I, the Lord, am your God
who led you forth from Egypt:
open wide your mouth,
and I will fill it.

—Psalm 81:11

ZACHARY

My Abba Bearer

awning, as his Miraculous Medal glittered outside his shirt, he came strutting into the sacristy. "Hi, I'm Father Zach, the new kid on the block."

"Hi, I'm Father Chris, the old kid on the block." Showing him the medal around my neck, I said, "Look, just like yours."

"Yes, indeed, she's the way to the 'Way'." Placing his finger on my medal, he asked, "What's this?"

As I looked down, his finger shot up and hooked my nose, slinging my head back. "Gotcha, lad!"

Still amused, I said, "I hear you're a Benedictine monk."

"That's right, I'm a monk, but don't put an 'e-y' on the end of it and make a 'monk**ey**' out of me," he said.

"You mean like you just did me?" He nodded his grin. "I won't, Father," I promised.

"Please, call me Zach."

"And you call me Chris."

"You're *Christopher* to me, laddy."

Finding out what I liked, Father Zach got two apples on a stick. In the garden—where Sister Amez had released that monarch butterfly to a new life—we sat face-to-face in a swing built for two. As we were swinging, he handed me one of the apples.

"Thank you," I said, "I never refuse an apple." Holding it, I sang, "I wish I had an apple on a stick, an apple on a stick, an apple on a stick."

He smiled and asked, "Why do you wish for something you already have?"

"Because, I didn't taste it yet, I guess."

"Then bite into it, lad, and fulfill your desire."

As I bit the apple it split in two. Peanut butter was in the place of the core. "Ha! Zach, how'd ya do it?"

"My secret is my secret." Enjoying my delight, he added, "The best is *within*."

"I'll say," I blurted out, enjoying the peanut butter.

The next day, he gave me a gift, saying, "*Christopher*, this is yours."

"What is it?"

"Open it and see; the best is within."

Receiving the present, I tore the wrapping to pieces, amusing my new friend. It was a framed saying:

> Priest of God, say this Mass
>   As if it were your First Mass,
> As if it were your last Mass,
>   As if it were your only Mass.

"O Zach, thanks! It'll be hung in the sacristy where it will remind me to pray the Mass with my whole heart, like you."

"That's the spirit, lad," he said. "And remember the Christ, 'the best within.'"

"O, now I got it!" I said.

"*Hooray, Christopher,*" he exclaimed. Placing his finger on my chest and pressing the medal under my shirt, he asked, "What's this, lad?"

Covering my nose, I said, "O no! Fool me once, shame on you; fool me twice, shame on me."

"I'm not trying to fool you, lad, but to make you realize that Jesus, the best, really lives within you," he said, pressing the medal harder on my heart. "Christopher, thou art the *Christ Bearer.*"

"And thou, Zachary, art my *Abba Bearer.*"

Through the three years of his residing at Holy Family Home, he taught me like Jesus taught His disciples. We were father and son. He was my confidant, confessor, and spiritual director. He taught me all about the Christ within me. Daily, I saw him in chapel totally absorbed in God, especially, before, during, and after the Holy Sacrifice of the Mass.

One evening, the night before my vacation, we sat again in the swing—our spiritual meeting place—under the crescent moon. I could tell that he wasn't feeling well, yet he never complained. Gliding back and forth, I thought about Yoey and her big wow.

"Zach, look!" I said, pointing to the quarter-moon. "God's thumb nail sticking out."

Like her, he exclaimed, "Wow!"

Feeling God close to me, I said, "Please, Father, hear my confession?"

"Sure," he said.

We stopped swinging and I began, "Bless me, Father, for I have sinned. It's a week since my last confession, and these are my sins: impatience, especially in traffic; doing my will, instead of His; I'm proud at times, self-righteous, and stubborn; also I lack trust in God. I'm sorry for all my sins, especially for being afraid of His will."

"O lad, be not afraid of His will; be afraid of yours." he said. "Pray not only for His will but also that His will embraces you. He'll never hurt you; He loves you with His whole heart ... What frightens you so much?"

"It's ... death."

"By golly, lad, I fretted it, too. But no more," he said.

"You did?" He nodded. "What took that monster away?" I asked.

"God, Himself, set me free from the hunter's snare."

"How?"

"Well, one day at Mass when I was covering for you, I had forgotten to pick up the chalice and consecrate the wine. Afterwards, in the sacristy, Sister Amez told me about it. 'O my!' I said. All day I worried about the validity of that Mass. That same night the Lord God revealed Himself to me in a dream and took away my fears."

"Please, tell me your dream."

After a reverent pause, he began:

Not knowing how, I found myself kneeling in the sanctuary, wearing my black habit and no shoes or socks. I was praying the rosary and meditating on the third glorious mystery, the Descent of the Holy Spirit, when suddenly golden light shone from the tabernacle upon me, piercing my hands, feet, and side.

And then, the Father of fathers appeared at the foot of the altar, surrounded by angels. He wore a white robe with a golden sash around His waist; white hair and beard. He focused His blue eyes on the altar. I figured, He wanted me to celebrate the Mass again and correct my mistake by consecrating the wine this time.

Rushing past Him and His angels to the sacristy, I found the door locked. Now what? I thought. How can I celebrate the Eucharist without my vestments, the bread and wine, sacred vessels, and Mass books? Where's the altar server? I wondered. My heart pounded and blood oozed from my stigmata. Throwing up my bleeding hands, in the reverence of the bowing angels, I peeked at the heavenly Father for help.

Smiling and winking at me, He opened His arms, saying, "Zachary, my son, come to Me."

*With no fuss, no ritual, in the form of a cross, I stretched out my bloody hands. Scuffling my wounded feet, I approached the Almighty One—only because I knew the presence of the saving Christ, **the best within me**. As I fell into the Father's embrace, all the angels disappeared, and He faded into my being. My heart radiated divinity, melting away all my anxieties, worries, and fears, especially over death—that Big Bad Wolf!*

Beyond the vestments, the vessels, and the ritual, I experienced the essence of the Holy Sacrifice of the Mass—God Himself—with burning love, WITHIN me, beyond all telling!

"Wow, hmm, how come I can't dream like that?"

"You will," he said as if prophesying. "For your penance, lad, pray the prayer for Blessed Jeanne Jugan's intercession for your special intention."

"I always do before Mass."

"Then make it part of your night prayer," he said. "Now make your act of contrition."

"O my God, I'm heartily sorry...."

After the absolution, he gave me a bear hug, saying, "Enjoy

your vacation and remember, Father Christopher, 'Thou art the *Christ Bearer*.'"

"And thou art my *Abba Bearer*," I whispered.

Towards the end of my vacation week, on the Feast of the Sacred Heart of Jesus, Father Zach was dying. I was at the shore when I got the call from Sister Amez.

"Father Chris," she said, "Father Zach was rushed to Mercy Hospital. He suffered a severe stroke during the Mass, after the consecration and right before *the elevation of the cup*." I remembered his dream. "It's serious; you better come."

"OK, I'm on my way."

Driving to the hospital seemed like an eternity. When I finally arrived, I got out of my car and my little Saint Joseph medal fell out of my pocket. Picking it up, I kissed the image of the patron saint of the dying and believed that he was going to die a blessed death. Inside the hospital, I stopped at the chapel for the Blessed Sacrament.

Gathered around Father Zach were Mother Vincent, Sister Amez, his nurse, and the doctor. Connected to a monitor, he drifted in and out of consciousness. His miraculous medal hung dangling off the guardrail of his bed, sparkling in the sun. Grasping it, I prayed, "O Mary conceived without sin pray for *him* who *has* recourse to you." Squeezing the medal with one hand and my little Saint Joseph with the other, I asked, "Has he been anointed?"

"Yes, Father, this morning," the nurse answered.

"Well, I'll anoint him again," I said, remembering my priesthood. I took my oils and placed the holy pyx—that moveable tabernacle—containing the Most Blessed Sacrament, on the blue blanket covering him. We sang *O Sacrament Most Holy*. After caressing his forehead and the **back** of his hands with the consecrated oil, I prayed the Apostolic pardon and made the sign of the cross over him with the pyx.

As for me, I could only see the Lord Jesus Christ crucified, suffering *within* Father Zach. His eyes rolled, his body squirmed, he gulped air, and as if on a cross, he pushed himself up and down to breathe.

Father Paul, the chaplain joined us. "Let's pray the rosary," he suggested. While we were praying the fifth sorrowful mystery, our beloved priest fixed his glazed eyes above us. We paused. In my heart, I prayed, "Father, Thy will be done."

"Blessed Mother…" he slurred, surprising us. A few times he bowed his head as though he were agreeing with someone. As he fell back on his pillow, we resumed praying the rosary.

The numbers on the monitor dropped low. The up-and-down vertical zigzag lines turned into perfect passing M's. When Father Paul began the Hail Holy Queen, Father Zach stopped breathing. Suddenly, at the words *show unto us the blessed fruit of your womb, Jesus,* my Abba took two last breaths. The horizontal line flattened. It was finished!

Gradually, a golden aura appeared around his face and a sweet fragrance filled the room. In my tears, I believed that my Abba took his place in heaven, praying—like all the other graduates—for my dream intention. Sister Amez poked me out of my teary daze.

"Another graduate, Father, with flying colors."

"*Summa Cum Laude*," I moaned, knowing our loss and heaven's gain.

"Let's go on for God," Mother said.

"Yes, let's, we may not be long for this world," Sister Amez responded.

"Hey, that's my line," I said.

Remembering Father Zach's dream and his last words to me "Thou art the *Christ Bearer*" that confessional night under the crescent moon, I gazed at his glowing face, whispering, "Thou art *my Abba Bearer.*"

Abba, Father, all things are possible to you.
Take this cup away from me,
but not what I will but what you will.

—Mark 14: 36

Epilogue

I t was the first day of summer, again. My 18th anniversary at
Holy Family Home. Ready for bed, I sang *Come Holy Ghost*. Ending
the hymn and grateful for my long assignment with the Little
Sisters, I gazed through my window and feasted my eyes on the
twinkling stars above. "My God how great Thou art!" I proclaimed.

That holy night, I could sense that something wonderful was
about to happen. In bed, I clutched my ruby rosary, whispered
the Blessed Jeanne Jugan intercessory prayer, and fell asleep.
FINALLY, I got my dream:

> *Sister Amez—in my dream and on my 'Watch'—sat by
> my death bed. I heard her whisper the Fifth Decade of Light:
> 'The Paschal Mystery and the Institution of the Holy
> Eucharist.' Before beginning the decade, she prayed the last
> words of her foundress for me: 'Eternal Father, open your
> gates today for Father Christopher who greatly longs to see
> you... O Mary, our dear mother, come to him. You know
> that he loves you and that he longs to see you.'*
>
> *I tried to talk, but couldn't. I wanted to say, 'Hey, I'm
> not ready yet.'*

Vanishing away from her to a dream within a dream, I found myself on a mountaintop under an apple tree, wearing my First Holy Communion suit. I was age 7 in body, but age 57 in my mind. At that moment, the Blessed Mother appeared to me hiding something behind her back. She wore a white gown, white mantle, blue veil, and a blue sash. Her countenance radiated my white clothes.

'Christopher, come closer,' she said.

'Wow,' I exclaimed, 'you know my name and you're more beautiful than I ever imagined.'

As I stepped in front of her, she draped my shoulders with her mantle. Stooping, she crowned me with a kiss. 'You're mine', she said. Revealing her hidden hand, she offered me an apple. 'It has peanut butter in it.'

'No thanks.'

'But you never refuse an apple.'

'I know, but I want more.'

'What?'

'The fruit of your wound.'

Smiling, she faded away and the Lord Jesus appeared right in front of me in my adult body, wearing an alb and a red sash, just as He had appeared on Sister Amez's Bible. Having my older voice, He asked, 'What's up, little brother?'

'Lord, am I dying?'

'What's this?' He asked pressing on the medal under my shirt.

Looking down, I said, 'It's my Miraculous—'

His finger shot up, hooking my nose, slinging my head back. 'Gotcha, lad,' he said, laughing. 'Follow me.'

Trudging behind Him, we stopped at the edge of the mountain. By His side, I saw an angel holding the end of a rope. Across the chasm of the next mountain, I saw another angel holding the other end. Pulling hard, the angels tightened the rope as the Lord hopped up and pranced on it, like a tightrope walker. 'Come to Me'. He said.

'Not out there, Lord.'

Grinning, Jesus pointed down. As quick as a blink, I was 'out there' on the limb with Him—unlike an acrobat, feeling awkward and afraid. I could smell something burning. I looked over to the other mountain and saw a volcano spitting out lava. Lowering my eyes and feeling the heat, I saw fiery fluids flowing down the rocks onto the river surface.

'Lord, save me!'

'Fall with me.'

'I'm afraid!'

'SURRENDER, CHRISTOPHER!'

'OK! Save me!'

Letting go of the rope, the angels flapped their wings and watched us twirling down in slow motion. As the flames below got closer, I bellowed, 'Lord, blow out the fire.' With a whirlwind breath, He blew the fire away but also the river, making a rocky desert below us. 'Quick!' I pleaded. 'Inhale and bring back the water.' Was this my purgatory? I wondered. Shutting my eyes and grinding my teeth, I felt a safe landing. 'Whew!' I sighed.

Opening my immortal eyes, I saw the suffering Christ dying in my 57-year-old body—in the form of a cross—smashed over the rugged rocks, gulping two last breaths. The pointed stones pierced my adult hands, feet, and side that Jesus possessed, bloodstaining His alb. I knew He had died my death.

Just then, from out of a rose-colored cloud, a voice proclaimed, 'You are my CHRISTOPHER. It pleases Me to give you the kingdom.'

Descending down farther, the divine cloud rested upon me. Light radiated from my hands, feet, and side, transfiguring me whiter than my communion suit. In the glorious glow of His saving presence, I buried my old Christ-like body under the rocky ground. Breaking a twig in two, I made a cross, blessed it, and stuck it into the rubble. Under the blue skies, I danced on my grave, singing, 'Who's Afraid of the Big Bad Wolf, the Big Bad Wolf, the Big Bad—'

Early in the morning on the first day of the week as the golden sun was rising and fading out the rose-tinted sky, the telephone rang—waking me to a new life.

"Good morning, this IS Father *Christopher*," I answered.

"Father *Christopher*?"

"That's right... O Mother, is someone *dying*?"

"Father, brace yourself." She paused. "Sister Amez died sometime during the night."

"O my... She's gone to her place in heaven. Another graduate," I said with the 'God Bumps' tingling within me.

"*Summa Cum Laude*," she said. "She didn't respond to her alarm clock. I just discovered her warm body beside her bed. From off the floor, I picked up her opened Bible. John 14:2-3 was highlighted... Father?"

"Yes, Mother?"

"You never know. Let's go on for God."

At the funeral Mass—her 'graduation ceremony'—I sprinkled Sister's coffin with holy water, praying, "In the waters of baptism, Sister Amez died with Christ and rose with Him to new life. May she now share with Him eternal glory."

Two Little Sisters draped the gray coffin with the white pall. Then Mother Vincent opened Sister Amez' Bible and placed it on that baptismal covering over the casket. I could hardly believe my gaping eyes—it was that same attractive Bible with the ascended Lord, wearing that alb and red sash around His waist, standing on those rose-tinted clouds in the midst of angelic trumpeters. It had been 18 years ago, almost to the day, when I first saw that glorious book and those highlighted words: John 14:3. Turning around, I processed down the aisle. The organ blasted and the choir sang out:

> *Be not afraid.*
> *I go before you always.*
> *Come follow me,*
> *And I will give you rest.*

As I relished the lyrics, I cried over the confirming hymn of my dream all the way down the aisle into the sanctuary. After the readings, I picked up Sister's Bible from off the casket, embracing that holy book. Standing near the flickering flame of the Paschal Candle in the glow of salvation, I solemnly proclaimed the highlighted Gospel that was already set like a seal on my heart, my priestly heart:

> *I am indeed going*
> *to prepare a place for you,*
> *and then I shall come back*
> *to take you with me,*
> *that where I am you also may be.*

At the grave site, after the burial rite, the Little Sisters sang the *Salve Regina*. When the Marian hymn ended, all departed in silence, except the cemetery workers, Abby with her funeral helpers (Jimmy and Johnny), the bobbing robins, the scampering squirrels, and me.

"This is Father Chris, the chaplain of Holy Family Home," Jimmy said, introducing me to the workers.

"Please call me, *Father Christopher*; I like it better."

"Better than this?" Johnny asked, tossing me an apple.

"You betcha!" I said, biting into it.

Between the grave diggers, I bowed peering down at the casket, noticing how its gray color darkened as it was being lowered into the bowels of the lightless earth. Suddenly and pleasantly distracted, I beheld a monarch butterfly, fluttering up out of the dismal hole. Plopping onto my index finger, it flapped its black and beautiful orange wings. Catching my breath, I stood up straight, watching it look at me. As I held it high, that marvelous creature flew into the blue skies towards the rose-tinted clouds. Just then, the chapel bells rang out. Dropping the apple core into the grave, I raised up my hands—with the 'God Bumps' reverberating all through me—and sang along with the melody of the chimes:

> *When Christ shall come with shout of acclamation*
> *And take me home what joy shall fill my heart!*
> *Then I shall bow in humble adoration,*
> *And there proclaim, my God how great thou art!*

In verdant pastures, I fixated upon a marble statue of the Risen Lord in the panoramic sunshine of all the tombstones, exclaiming, "O death, where *IS* your victory?" Mocking that 'Grim Reaper' one last time, I danced and sang, *Who's Afraid of the Big Bad Wolf, the Big Bad Wolf, the Big Bad Wolf?* Then, fearing no evil, I drove through Holy Cross Cemetery, exiting from the graveyard grounds of my mortal mind and entering into my immortal soul, *within* the One, Eternal, Triune God—no longer afraid anymore.

May the divine assistance remain always with us and may the souls of the faithful departed through the mercy of God rest in peace; especially, the *Summa Cum Laude* Graduates of Holy Family Home, our spiritual professors and guides to *Heaven's Homecoming*.

"Yes, I am coming soon."
Amen! Come, Lord Jesus!

—Revelation 22:20

Intercessory Prayer of Saint Jeanne Jugan

Jesus, You rejoiced and praised Your
Father for having revealed to the little ones
the mysteries of the Kingdom of Heaven.
We thank You for the graces granted to
Your humble servant, Jeanne Jugan, to
whom we confide our petitions and needs.

Father of the Poor, You have never
refused the prayer of the lowly. We ask
You, therefore, to hear the petitions that
she presents to You on our behalf.

Jesus, through Mary, Your Mother and
ours, we ask this of You, who lives and
reigns with the Father and the Holy Spirit
now and forever. Amen.

SAINT JEANNE JUGAN
FOUNDRESS OF THE LITTLE SISTERS OF THE POOR
(1792-1879)
CANONIZED OCTOBER 11, 2009

ABOUT THE AUTHOR

Father Douglas McKay was ordained in 1982 for the Archdiocese of Philadelphia. As a priest, he has ministered in parishes, hospitals, prisons, schools, neighborhood bars, playgrounds, and on the streets. Since 1993, he has been the chaplain of Holy Family Home, serving the elderly with the Little Sisters of the Poor. He is also the Founder and Chaplain of Our House Ministries, Inc., an Addiction Resource Center, established in 1997 in the Grays Ferry section of the city in addition to serving as Chaplain of the Calix Society, Philadelphia Unit, that proclaims the Catholic faith to the Alcoholics Anonymous membership. Father resides at Holy Family Home.